THE HEALER

A Doctor's Crusade Against Addiction and AIDS

BENY J. PRIMM, MD

WITH JOHN S. FRIEDMAN

Foreword by David Dinkins

D1445802

ISBN: 1499547978
ISBN 13: 9781499547979

Library of Congress Control Number: 2014908941
CreateSpace Independent Publishing Platform
North Charleston, South Carolina

Nonetheless, he knew that the tale he had to tell could not be one of final victory. It could only be the record of what had had to be done...by all who, while unable to be saints but refusing to bow down to pestilences, strive their utmost to be healers.

Albert Camus,
The Plague

Contents

Acknowledgments

Space does not permit naming everyone to whom I owe gratitude. I express my deepest appreciation to all who worked for me at the Addiction Research and Treatment Corporation (ARTC) and the Urban Resource Institute (URI). In particular, I want to thank my longtime assistant Maxine Dotson; our attorney Tom Rafalsky; former senior vice president and later chief executive officer Dr. Lawrence Brown; senior vice presidents Eddie Lightsey, Robert Sage, and Deborah Wright; vice presidents Angela Grant and Renee Sumpter; chief financial officer Sam Duvoor; and key personnel, past and present: Faziela Bacchus, Chuck Bailey, the late Louis Bingham, Roosevelt Dulaurier, Richard Gaffney, Dr. Carlotta John-Hull, Karl Jones, Anthony Mcleod, and Madeleine Miller. The board members to whom I owe special gratitude include a founder of ARTC, Horace Morancie and original URI board member Carmen Smith; Juan Bailey, Vivian Bright, Corinna Grant, Joyce Hall, Bridget McCray, and Judy Mitchell. Of those who served with me in Washington, DC, special thanks to Sue Becker, Warren Hewitt, Lisa Scheckel Levy, and Robert Lubran.

Dr. Jerome Jaffe and his wife Faith have been lifelong friends and mentors. Other colleagues who have been greatly supportive include Dr. Robert Dupont, Dr. Herbert Kleber, Dr. Mary Jeanne Kreek, and Dr. Edward Senay.

I also thank (and to acknowledge the memory of, where appropriate) Calvin Anderson, Cornelius Baker, Dr. Patricia Bath, Romare Bearden, Martha Duncan Bond, the late Samuel Brisbane, Gloria Primm Brown, Reverend Calvin O.Butts III, the late Dr. Herbert Cave, Dr. Wesley Clark, the late Dr. Vincent Cordice, Sy Demsky, David Dinkins, Joseph Drew, Marcielle Ellis, Dr. Ralph Fenderson, C. Virginia Fields, Nathaniel Fields, Loretta Finnegan, Dr. Ginger Davis Floyd, Dr. Frank Fraser, Debra Frazer-Howze, Dr. Melissa Freeman, Dr. Tom Friedan, Henry Louis Gates, Dr. Helene Gayle, June Mitchell Glover, Sheila Harley, Ernest Hopkins, Jada Hunter, Earvin "Magic" Johnson, the late Dr. Alexander Jordan,

Dr. Natalie Kanem, Paul Kawata, Edythe London, Dr. Joyce Lowinson, Charles Madry, the late Ira Marion, Dr. John Martin, the late Dr. Thomas Matthew, Doug Michaels, Dr. Robert Newman, Mark Parrino, Dr. Fred Parrott, the late Basil Paterson, David Paterson, Dr. Lucy Perez, Paul Perito, Muriel Pettione, John Phillips, Dr. James Robinson, Dr. David Satcher, Reverend Edwin Saunders, the late Robert Schuster, Pernessa Seale, Gloria Searson, Dr. Louis Sullivan, the late Percy Sutton, Dr. Zelalem Temesgen, Harold Trigg, Debra Wafer, the late Dr. Charles Wilson, Phil Wilson, the late Judge Bruce Wright, Kathy Yee, Robert Yearwood; Congresswoman Donna Christensen, Congressman Elijah Cummings, Congressman Charles Rangel, Congressman Louis Stokes, Congressman Edolphus Towns, Congresswoman Maxine Waters, State Senator William Perkins, State Senator Ruth Hassel Thompson, Assemblyman Keith Wright.

I want to honor the memory of the late Barbara Gibson and the late Gerome Primm.

Above all, I am grateful for the devotion of my beloved late wife, Annie Delphine Evans Primm. My love and gratitude go to my daughters Annelle, Martine, Jeanine, and Eraka Fortuit; my granddaughters, India Delphine Primm-Spencer and Noa Fortuit.

And finally, my deepest appreciation and love to my fiancée, Ellena Stone Huckaby, for her unconditional love and support of my life's work.

Beny J. Primm, MD

I thank all my colleagues and the secretary in the American Studies/Media and Communications Department at the College at Old Westbury, the State University of New York and my former colleague Rosalyn Baxandall. I also thank Arts and Sciences Dean Barbara Hillery and Provost and Vice President for Academic Affairs Patrick O'Sullivan.

My thanks to Harold and Sally Burman, Mark Carlson, Rebecca Friedman Clapham, Kevin Clapham, Michael Cousins, Ariel and Angelica Dorfman, Shakun Drew, Hamilton Fish, Richard and Sylvia Fox,

Ellen Hinsey, Cathy Lace, Brenda Levin, Dr. George Lombardi, Hugh Mackenzie, Richard McCord, Roger Salloch, Herta Schuster, Maria Solomon, and Barbara Solomon.

My special gratitude to Joseph Drew for five decades of friendship.

Above all, I want to thank my daughter, Julia, for her invaluable suggestions and encouragement and my wife, Kathleen McCaffrey Friedman, without whose patience, helpful advice, and comprehensive editing this book would not have been possible.

John S. Friedman

Foreword

In the early 1980s, I was New York City Clerk overseeing, among other things, the Marriage Bureau. One day, we received a letter from a man, terminally ill with AIDS, who wanted to get married before he died but was unable to come to our office to file an application for a license. Typically, when an applicant was incapacitated, a clerk would visit the home or hospital to help complete forms. In this instance, however, none of the staff was willing to go, so I myself went to the hospital that day. It was my first experience with someone suffering from AIDS, and it was the last time anyone in the City Clerk's office refused to help someone with the disease.

At that time, HIV/AIDS was thought to afflict only gay white men, a misimpression that persisted long after Surgeon General C. Everett Koop issued a warning in 1987 about the disproportionately high rate of infection among African Americans. Some heard the warning and its implications for the African American community—among them, Dr. Beny Primm. That same year, he and Debra Fraser-Howze helped to found the National Black Leadership Commission on AIDS (NBLCA), which has become one of the leading organizations in the fight against the epidemic within the black population.

Dr. Primm could see, even then, what disastrous consequences our community faced if people continued to ignore the warning, and he was determined to educate the public about the disease before the epidemic gained force.

While chair of the board of the NBLCA from 1998 to 2004, I took my cues from a small group, one of whom was Beny Primm. During my first year as chair, he played a pivotal role in persuading the Clinton administration to declare the AIDS epidemic a state of crisis and to make available $156 million to fund AIDS programs designed to serve at-risk minority populations, the first of continuing annual grants.

Beny's role as a general in the fight against HIV/AIDS in the early years of the epidemic cannot be overstated. When activists protested at government meetings and public forums, he lent a gravitas that gave credence to the sense of urgency. His knowledge and willingness to listen to different voices earned him the admiration of street people as well as of four US presidents who appointed and reappointed him as their advisor.

I have known Beny as a friend and professional since the early 1950s in Harlem. I recall attending meetings together in the early 1970s, convened by Dr. M. Moran Weston, the pastor of Saint Philips Church in Harlem and a founder of the Carver Federal Savings Bank. About fifteen people attended the monthly breakfast meetings, which brought together some of New York's leading black professionals. Beny was a member, and I knew I had arrived when I was invited into a group of that caliber.

Over the decade during which I was Manhattan Borough president and New York City mayor, Beny was a key consultant on HIV/AIDS and substance abuse issues. One of the controversial subjects at the time was needle exchange, a way to prevent HIV/AIDS infection from spreading through the practice of sharing syringes. Initially, I scoffed at the notion of giving needles to addicts, but Beny convinced me, and others who were equally skeptical, that needle exchange would curb the spread of the disease, and there is now evidence that it has. Beny was also instrumental in persuading more than a few public officials to reconsider their objections to the use of methadone in treating drug addiction, which his organization, the Addiction Research and Treatment Corporation (ARTC), the largest, not-for-profit, minority-run drug treatment program in the nation, proved to be best practice.

The life of Beny Primm parallels the African American experience of the twentieth century. Having grown up in the segregated South, he with his family joined the Great Migration north in the early 1940s. Coming of age in the Bronx and Harlem, he attended black colleges, served in the segregated then desegregated army, and participated in the civil rights movement. His story is one of a generation of achievers who fought for the opportunity to pursue their goals while lifting others up with them. Beny's personal goal was to become a medical doctor and to develop a modern drug abuse treatment that would enable those trapped in addiction to ultimately follow their dreams as well.

The career of Beny Primm could have followed a different path. He might have set out to make millions. Instead, he chose to work for the fortuneless and the forgotten and, in so doing, created national models of care that have helped thousands emerge from the darkness of addiction and the pain of pandemic illness. We are in his debt for putting the needs of others above his own, for giving higher priority to doing good rather than doing well.

David Dinkins

Chapter One

The Responsible Revolutionary

So early in my life, I had learned that if you want something, you had better make some noise.

Malcolm X, *The Autobiography of Malcolm X*

A week after John F. Kennedy announced his candidacy for the presidency of the United States, and a few weeks before four students sat down at a Woolworth's in Greensboro, North Carolina, I began my internship in January 1960 at Meadowbrook Hospital (now Nassau County General Hospital) on Long Island. A year later I became the hospital's first resident in anesthesia and passed my state medical board exam.

Obstetrics and gynecology had been my first choice—but then race relations intervened. I heard white women object to the idea of "a black guy delivering my baby." This situation became real to me one winter night early in my career as an intern when a woman stumbled into the emergency room at Long Island's Good Samaritan Hospital complaining of wrenching abdominal pain and vaginal bleeding.

"You'll have to be examined," I said.

"I don't want that nigger to touch me," she snapped at the nurse.

"Well," I said, "you could die from internal bleeding if you have a ruptured ectopic pregnancy. You must be seen soon. Otherwise, I'm going to my quarters to sleep."

After a minute, she relented.

I experienced this often as a new doctor in the early 1960s. And it wasn't in Mississippi. It was in the Long Island suburbs of New York City.

John Anderson, then a nurse anesthetist at Meadowbrook Hospital, explained that "the community of Levittown contiguous to the hospital was lily-white, and that attitude was reflected at the hospital where only 3 or 4 percent of the staff were nonwhite. In the department of anesthesiology, there was a fellow from India, one black in the orthopedic department, and one or two in the department of medicine. Overall, the staff was predominantly white, though the hospital was a public hospital for the poor. Beny became the first black resident in anesthesiology, a trailblazer, and an example to others."

I had applied for an externship at the Methodist Hospital in Brooklyn, where I knew there were no black doctors. This was the very hospital that received generous contributions from Saint Mark's Methodist Church where I had practically lived while growing up in New York, and where my mother had tithed. Her father, my namesake, had been a Methodist minister. This history connected me in my heart and mind to these institutions, so it was a bitter realization that skin color could trump all. It was not to be.

Instead, I found myself in an internship and residency at Meadowbrook from 1960 to 1963. During that period I also worked as an emergency room doctor and anesthesiologist at a number of Long Island hospitals, including Good Samaritan in West Islip; Brunswick Hospital Center in Amityville; Whitestone Hospital in Whitestone, Queens; and Oyster Bay Hospital in Oyster Bay.

As an anesthesiologist, I soon realized that putting someone to sleep could move that person close to death. One slip and the patient could be gone. Fortunately, I never slipped. But once, while training at Meadowbrook, a surgeon operating on an athlete who was an Olympic hopeful clipped the man's aorta with a clamp, and blood shot up to the ceiling. Tragically, there wasn't enough blood typed and matched on hand to save the young man. That was the only death on the table in all my experience, and I've anesthetized thousands of patients.

In the early 1960s, I was usually on for thirty-six hours and off for twelve at the various places where I worked. The hours were long and the salary meager during this period. I earned just three dollars an hour and took home even less, since as a private contractor, I was charged by some of the hospitals for use of the equipment—an item also billed to the patient and/or the insurance company.

In 1963, I began a full-time position at Harlem Hospital in trauma anesthesia. My shifts ran from 4:00 p.m. on Friday through Sunday morning, a block of time when many cases required emergency surgery. One night, we had a man who was bleeding to death from a gunshot wound. Rushed to the OR, he was also found to have a year-old stab wound to the heart. I read his old chart and saw that he was an addict. After further study, I realized that almost 90 percent of the emergency surgery at Harlem Hospital on the weekends was associated either directly or indirectly with narcotic addiction.

Drug addiction, a citywide social and medical problem, had also become a contentious political issue. In his 1966 New York gubernatorial reelection campaign, Nelson Rockefeller demanded an "all-out war on drugs and addiction." In speech after speech, he asserted that the election of his Democratic opponent, City Council President Frank O'Connor, "would mean narcotic addicts would continue to be free to roam the street—to mug, snatch purses, to steal, even to murder, or to spread the deadly infection that afflicts them possibly to your own son or daughter. Half the crime in New York City is committed by narcotic addicts."

By such fear mongering, Rockefeller hardened his law-and-order image to meet the political requirements of his party and tried to show that he had the experience to solve the nationwide menace of drug abuse. After his election, Rockefeller pushed a law through the state legislature providing for the involuntary confinement of drug addicts for "treatment"—even if they were not convicted of a crime. If someone was found using drugs, he could be committed for up to three years; someone who had committed a felony while under the influence of drugs could be sentenced for up to five years on the drug charge alone.

In a policy euphemistically called "civil commitment," addicts were involuntarily committed and locked up in "rehabilitation centers." Parents could commit their children simply by making a statement that they were using drugs. Of course, they expected their sons and daughters to be assigned to plush rehab facilities. Mothers, fathers, boyfriends, and girlfriends became informants, and the police went to homes and forced the unwilling relative or friend into the program. Parents didn't know that they were sending their children to jail. The Rockefeller program was imprisoning people who were innocent.

Thought of as treatment, it was anything but that. There were no facilities. The so-called treatment was administered at state prisons—Attica, Woodhaven, and elsewhere. Former prison guards became rehabilitation officers, actually performing counseling and custodial tasks. It is an understatement to say that they were inadequately trained for these positions. An environment of harsh discipline failed to offer therapeutic benefits or lead to behavioral change. Nor was a distinction made between those prisoners who had committed serious offenses and those who had volunteered to participate in the Rockefeller drug program, which lasted for about three years. It was a complete and utter failure.

Danny Cook, whom I met in the 1960s and eventually hired, had worked for New York State as an induction officer in Harlem, sending addicts to prison. He later remembered what happened to a friend of his under the Rockefeller program: "He was in his 40's and didn't want to use drugs anymore and under no circumstances did he want to go back to the Dannemora penitentiary [the Clinton Correctional Facility in Dannemora, New York]. I saw him one day on 125th street and he told me: 'I'm hooked up now. I joined the state [Rockefeller] program.' My knees buckled. I wanted to cry. The next week he was shipped back to Dannemora. He probably committed suicide in that place."

As an anesthesiologist, I saw young people in the ER, their bodies riddled with bullet and knife wounds. I knew that behind this devastation was the scourge of drugs, and I made a promise to myself that I would work to stop these black kids from going down. I promised myself that, from that point on, I would do everything in my power to liberate my people from this terrible affliction. That decision marked one of the turning points in my life.

In early 1964, I wrote a paper for my supervisors suggesting that everyone coming into the hospital, regardless of their medical or surgical diagnosis, be screened for substance abuse problems. I recommended that they should be interviewed in a hospital setting, where they might be more open and receptive to receiving help and, when indicated, be placed on a course of drug abuse treatment. As there was an affiliation at the time between Harlem Hospital and Columbia University, the dean of the medical school, Dr. Melvin Lahr, read my paper and suggested that I try to implement the strategy. He spoke on my behalf to Dr. Herbert Cave, my immediate superior and head of anesthesiology at Harlem as well as an eminent physician and civil rights leader. The first black diplomat of the American Academy of Anesthesiology, Cave was a member of the medical team that operated on Martin Luther King Jr. for a chest wound after he was stabbed at Harlem's Blumstein Department Store in 1958. Dr. Cave had also participated as a medic in the nonviolent demonstrations in Mississippi in 1964 and in the fifty-four-mile march from Selma to Montgomery in 1965.

Dr. Cave considered me his protégé and appreciated my innovations at Harlem Hospital. (I had, for example, helped organize a resuscitation plan—Code 777, now called code blue—for a patient undergoing cardiac arrest.) Dr. Cave was in full agreement with my proposal that anyone admitted to the hospital with a substance abuse problem should be encouraged to enter a drug abuse program as part of treatment. As a result, I oversaw the opening of the Hospital Orientation Center and became head of its Narcotics Control Program in 1964, funded by the city's Addiction Services Agency. The program was created from scratch in a closet that reeked of disinfectant, with one assistant and a secretary. Our first task was to identify patients in need. I also created a group called the Council of Community Voices on Narcotics based at Harlem Hospital to draw public attention to drug abuse and to agitate for additional funds and services. There were meetings, protests, and rallies. One Saturday, protestors marched to the hospital where they knew that the eighth floor was basically empty. I got a call at home to come to the hospital, where about fifty people were sitting in, refusing to budge until services were provided. I met with them that day and again on Sunday morning.

Among their chief complaints was that Harlem and other black communities were receiving only a trickle of the $29 million granted by the legislature for the state and city narcotics programs that year. "We've got so many addicts up here that even the buildings are nodding," one man said. As spokesman for the group, I was quoted in the *New York Times*: "There is only one rehabilitation center in Harlem...[yet] this is the largest area of narcotics addiction in the world." The State of New York sent Samuel Singletary (a special assistant to Governor Rockefeller) who told the protestors that their "beefs" were legitimate and that he would pass along their complaints to the governor. Fortunately, he made a tactical error by promising state funding if the hospital allowed the group to stay. Two or three months later, the funds arrived, and the group, called the People's Program, stayed on the eighth floor for a year. I appeared on television requesting volunteers for the operation, and physicians and nurses donated their time.

In early 1966, I received a phone call from Thomas Matthew, a doctor-activist who had heard about my drug abuse work, perhaps through his wife, Carol Lewis, whom I had known during my teenage years at Saint Mark's Church. We met, and Tom proposed that I join him at a hospital in Queens that he was about to open. At first I was reluctant because of my full schedule, but I soon fell under the spell of his magnetism. In any case, I was grateful for the opportunity to work with him in the black community he was serving.

Described by the *New York Times* as "an inexhaustible activist, with the zeal of a country preacher and the vocabulary of a scholar," Tom Matthew was born in New York City in 1924 as one of eight children. His father was a janitor. After graduating from the Bronx High School of Science, Manhattan College, and Meharry Medical College in 1949, he trained in St. Louis, Cleveland, and Boston before returning to New York as the first trained African American neurosurgeon. Though he never passed the specialty boards in neurosurgery, he was given a neurosurgeon's rating by the State Workmen's Compensation Board and Health Insurance Plan of Greater New York (HIP). During the mid-1950s, he developed a neurosurgery department at Sydenham Hospital in Harlem where, according to his daughter, Laura, he was shocked by the horrible conditions that any doctor who worked in the inner city would see.

Leaving Sydenham, Tom became director of neurosurgery at Coney Island Hospital from 1956 to 1962. Then in 1966, with initial funding from churches as well as from Jewish and Italian groups, he purchased a fading orange-brick building formerly owned by HIP at 175-10 88th Avenue in Jamaica, Queens (doing much of the repair work himself) and established the foundation of what would become Interfaith Hospital, focusing on chronic care. Offering geriatric and pediatric care as well as general surgery, the hospital had about 150 beds. Tom believed that I could put my own growing experience in drug abuse treatment to good use at Interfaith.

By 1964, Harlem had become the drug capital of America, with a drug addiction rate ten times higher than the New York City average and twelve times higher than the United States as a whole. Still, drug treatment facilities were few and far between. Beth Israel Medical Center at First Avenue and 16th Street in Manhattan, called Manhattan General, was the city's primary facility—with a two-year waiting list and fewer than twenty-five beds in early 1966 for all of Manhattan. In an attempt to bypass this bottleneck, I recruited Danny Cook as a drug abuse counselor and opened a detoxification program at Interfaith Hospital for heroin patients. He had seen first-hand the devastation caused by the Rockefeller program, and I had come to know him as compassionate and streetwise. Danny was to become my friend and confidant.

Detoxification, a process by which the body frees itself of a drug and its toxins while symptoms of withdrawal are treated simultaneously, is the primary step in any drug treatment program. As the body recovers from substance dependence, the goal immediately becomes long-term abstinence, which is best attained in a community residential treatment program or in outpatient drug treatment lasting from three to six months or longer.

Our program eventually became the main source of patients and income at Interfaith Hospital, and we became known citywide. But we were desperate for supplies, so Danny and I paid a visit to the federal government's accounting office. The official at the desk was popping nitroglycerin tablets into his mouth during our meeting, prompting me to whisper to Danny, "Let's get this thing done before he dies." In any case, the gentleman gave us carte blanche to take supplies from a defense department warehouse at Fort Hamilton in Brooklyn, where we found much needed hospital beds, cots, etc., and nicely outfitted the hospital.

At first, I combined weekends at Harlem Hospital with weekdays at Interfaith, eventually becoming full time at Interfaith to manage the detoxification program while working as second-in-command under Tom. Soon realizing that detox was only the first step, we developed an innovative, sociopsychological concept of changing lives. Following detox, according to our plan, addicts needed to become free of drugs and secure training, jobs, and places to live—a concept far more holistic and patient centered than nearly any other program in existence. This "supermarket" approach, as I then termed it, formed the cornerstone of my treatment philosophy.

Interfaith soon became one of the largest providers of treatment for addicts in the city. Our services were in demand, and our capacity was often stretched thin. Days were long; we began our admissions at 4:00 a.m.

Still, I wanted to establish a treatment facility in Harlem where the need was so great. The main program there at the time was the Addicts Rehabilitation Center, a drug-free (no methadone administered) facility begun in 1957 at the Manhattan Christian Reform Church by the Reverend Eugene Callender and later run by the Reverend James Allen, who himself had received treatment for drug abuse at a federal facility in Lexington, Kentucky.

The first obstacle to bringing treatment to Harlem was space. To say it was not readily available would be an understatement. Landlords and residents shared a Not in My Backyard Attitude (NIMBY) to drug abuse facilities. So, we began taking space. In March 1968, Tom and I and some fifty fatigue-clad helpers, many recovered or recovering drug addicts from Interfaith Hospital, cut through a padlocked chain with a pair of long-handled shears and quickly breached the doors of three vacant, dilapidated apartment buildings at 324, 344, and 346 Saint Nicholas Avenue in Harlem. Our purpose was to convert the contiguous buildings into a halfway house for drug addicts. When we arrived, reporters were waiting for us. Soon the police were sent to remove us from the building. Tom told them that the building was abandoned: "Girls can be dragged in here, and addicts use it to shoot up. We are taking this over." He added that, because the former owners had defaulted on taxes, the building was now owned by the city. The next day, believe it or not, we had the deed to the building. Our addicts now had a place to live, and we employed them to repair the space. This process had become a form of sit-in, of nonviolent protest.

At about the same time, we smuggled beds and other supplies into a half-empty state building on 125th Street and Lexington Avenue to set up a detox center. We were able to get into the building through the basement of a bookstore on the corner, run by an African Nationalist. (The bookstore was called UCLA—University at the Corner of Lenox Avenue.) Three weeks later, police officers arrived with Inspector Arthur Hill, the third highest black police official in New York City. His policemen, tall Nordic types, were heavily armed and wore helmets. As they entered the building and lined up, Hill said, "Take your people and walk out; don't harass the cops." If I refused, he said, he would arrest and handcuff me. Some of our people had bench warrants and would have faced long prison sentences. And so we left.

Later, on April 3, about ten of us outfitted in army fatigues burst into the fifteenth floor offices of the State Department of Social Services at 250 Broadway across from City Hall and held a sit-in to protest the non-reimbursement to Interfaith of $65,000 as a result of cuts to Medicaid by the state legislature. We took over the fifteenth floor and blocked all entrances, putting wedges into the elevator and chasing intruders away with fire extinguishers. Meals were prepared on hot plates. Several days later we permitted the office workers to return and allowed people with complaints to enter.

After a week, we grabbed papers off desks and threw them out the windows. It wasn't easy for me to protest in this manner. It went against the grain. I guess I didn't want to jeopardize my reputation. But I had learned from Tom that you have to disrupt to get the attention of the press and government officials. As we scattered the documents and they floated to the pavement on Broadway, the police who had been stationed in the lobby throughout this period saw them and rushed upstairs. I pulled the fire alarm, yelled fire, and we ran down the stairs and walked out through the front lobby. The only person arrested was one guy who took the elevator.

We also took over a building at 118th and Eighth Avenue, where I found myself on April 4, 1968, the night of the Martin Luther King assassination. It was colder than usual for early spring, and there was no heat in the building; so we had a fire going in a barrel, and a group of us stood around, blowing on our fingers. There was sporadic violence as gangs threw rocks, looted, and committed arson. Having come to Harlem to encourage calm, Mayor John Lindsay found himself caught in the middle of an unruly crowd and had to be hustled away by bodyguards.

As Danny recounted, "Some young white boy with no sense at all stopped his car at 118th street and Eighth Avenue. The crowd dragged him out of the car, leaving the door wide open. Dr. Primm grabbed one of the guys in the back of the group and said, 'I'm a doctor. Don't cut him.' He then grabbed the boy, put him back in the car, and watched him drive away. We could hear gunfire on the streets that night."

Four days later, Tom and a dozen men, again attired in army fatigues and soft-brimmed caps, forced their way into Governor Rockefeller's midtown Manhattan office and held a sit-in to protest, again, the state's failure to grant Medicaid funds to Interfaith. Reaching the foyer of the office, they were blocked by sixteen state troopers in plain clothes. At four o'clock in the afternoon, Jackie Robinson, at the time a special assistant to the governor for community affairs, informed Tom that the Department of Health had been asked to appoint an administrator to oversee Interfaith. Tom replied that he would be very happy to see a consulting administrator, as the hospital already had a de facto administrator—me.

Recognizing that other services were needed in the black community beyond Interfaith, Tom set up a parent company called the National Education Growth and Reconstruction Organization (NEGRO). He particularly wanted to assist blacks who had come north as part of the Great Migration but were largely unprepared for work in the cities. Noting the model of other immigrant groups—Jews, Irish, Italians—who were met by an established social matrix that supported them, he observed that blacks who had moved from the South lacked a similar network and had great need of one in the inner cities where social dislocation was profound. Simply traveling from one part of a city to another presented problems. Through NEGRO, Tom started the Blue & White Bus Line, a transportation service for Queens. He then initiated one for the Watts section of Los Angeles and another for Philadelphia, hiring former patients from Interfaith as drivers and maintenance men.

To fund services and to provide jobs, NEGRO obtained contracts from the Department of Defense to make belts and canteen covers for use in Vietnam. Its Freedom Village factory on 123rd street and Saint Nicolas Avenue, as well as small factories in Watts, Pittsburgh, and Washington, DC, also secured contracts to manufacture clothing and heat packs.

Tom put in a bid to the federal government for a contract to produce disinfectants for food and water purification in Vietnam. Dupont and Monsanto also bid. The first question government officials asked was, "Where's your factory?"

He said, "We don't have a factory."

The Defense Department officials said, "How then are you going to fulfill this contract?"

Tom answered, "You got a problem with black enterprise?"

Tom came home with the contract, and Dupont agreed to help provide equipment and personnel.

Struggling to focus greater attention on the problems around drug addiction in the black community, Tom and I had borrowed the nonviolent tactics of the civil rights movement, and to a lesser extent of the black power struggle. To avoid public attention, we met on a rooftop with Stokely Carmichael, the Trinidadian American activist who rose to prominence as a leader of the Student Nonviolent Coordinating Committee (SNCC) and later as the "honorary prime minister" of the Black Panther Party. We also met with H. Rap Brown, chairman of the SNCC in the 1960s, who, during a six-month alliance between SNCC and the Black Panther Party, served as the organization's minister of justice. Rap and Stokely wanted to express their solidarity with us, learn what we were doing, and determine how they might help. But nothing specific was ever agreed upon.

Tom also had discussions concerning the Watts bus operation in Los Angeles with Ron Karenga, a major figure in the black power movement, now best known for promoting the pan-African and African American holiday of Kwanzaa. And he met with Malcolm X, who tried to help NEGRO through the Organization of Afro-American Unity (OAAU), composed mainly of ex-Garveyites, proponents of Pan-Africanism who advocated a return to Africa by American blacks, and a departure from Africa of the European colonial powers. Unfortunately, the organization wasn't of much help to us.

As the black establishment didn't consider us radicals like Rap Brown or Carmichael, I was able to connect with Charlie Rangel, Adam Clayton Powell's successor as the democratic congressman from Harlem, and with Percy Sutton, who later became borough president of Manhattan. They were sympathetic to our goals, and my early meetings with them led to lifelong friendships and alliances.

For his part, Tom made connections to Richard Nixon through Nixon's aide Patrick Buchanan, who had introduced them when Nixon was practicing law in the mid-1960s in New York. Through his activities in Watts, Tom also developed a relationship with Robert Finch, lieutenant governor of California and later a close Nixon advisor who eventually became secretary of the Department of Health, Education, and Welfare. Nixon and Finch considered Tom a rising star among minority businessmen and in the world of black capitalism and gave their full support to NEGRO. For his efforts, Tom was able to obtain about $8.2 million from Medicaid, $2.4 million in defense contracts, $400,000 in bonds, and $227,000 from the Small Business Administration to keep Interfaith running and to support NEGRO.

In 1969, during Nixon's first year as president, Timothy Costello, a deputy New York City mayor, got a call "from somebody in the White House" who said that the president would be appreciative if Tom were not evicted from a building he had seized. Later, when New York City detectives were investigating Tom, Robert Finch stated that Nixon had personally ordered that "all assistance possible" be given to Tom. Finch added that to inform them of the president's wishes, he had subsequently held meetings with various government agencies, including Health, Education and, Welfare; Defense; and the Small Business Administration.

Tom also had the support of Governor Rockefeller. In 1972, Alton Marshall, a top aide to Rockefeller, intervened with the state health commissioner to keep Interfaith open despite inspection reports that detailed deteriorating health conditions, such as urine stains on the floors and patients sleeping without sheets on bare mattresses. A spokesperson for Rockefeller's state health commissioner told the*New York Times that* Rockefeller aides had "leaned over backwards to allow this facility to operate in view of the fact that it was the only black self-help facility in the state."

Despite the political support, the IRS pursued Tom for income tax evasion. After pleading guilty in 1969, he was sentenced to six months in prison but was pardoned by Nixon two months later. Tom finally lost the administration's support following a trip to Russia during the height of the Cold War; the Defense Department's contracts for the factory in Queens ceased. Then in 1972, Interfaith lost its state accreditation but stayed open for more than a year. Queens District Attorney Thomas Mackell went after Tom for "bookkeeping errors," according to Tom's daughter, Laura, and ordered his arrest in 1973. In December of that year, he was found guilty by the state supreme court of misapplying Medicaid funds and sentenced to three years in prison. Tom called the arrest "a political thing." In 1975, a Brooklyn appellate court struck down the conviction and dismissed all charges, stating, "There is not one fragment of testimonial or documentary evidence to suggest that the defendant acted with larcenous intent." The court agreed that Medicaid funds could be used for drug abuse treatment purposes—an important new ruling at the time.

"When Interfaith was shut as a drug treatment facility, my father personally assumed liability for NEGRO, about $2.5 million," recalled Laura. "And he let everybody go without any obligation." The building ultimately became a residence for children and was never utilized again as a hospital.

Some years later, Danny Cook remembers seeing Tom at Grand Central Station. He was working as a doctor on call for an agency, receiving a small fee for seeing patients. "He was disheveled. It tore me up to see him."

The first black person trained as a neurosurgeon in the United States, Tom Matthew died in 1996 in relative obscurity. He was a Bronx ghetto kid who became a passionate physician and committed activist. A brilliant and confrontational intellectual, his activism arose, as it did for others, from bitter experience of the establishment's assault on him and on the black community. But Tom was his own kind of revolutionary, unattached to any group or ideology.

Though our backgrounds were different, and despite his eventual financial and political woes, he was a significant mentor and role model for me. Because of him, I became more radical. Though his influence goes far beyond these words, he taught me, to paraphrase Malcolm X, that you have to make noise to make change.

Chapter Two

Into the Fray

———— ∞∞∞ ————

Heroin had just about taken over Harlem.... Every time I went
uptown somebody else was hooked, somebody else was strung
out.... You'd ask about an old friend, and they'd say, "Oh, well,
he's strung out." It wasn't just a comment or an answer to a
question. It was a eulogy for someone.

Claude Brown, *Manchild in the Promised Land*

In the spring of 1969, as Interfaith was slowly expiring, I received a
phone call from New York State Supreme Court Justice Edward
Dudley, who said he was working with Herbert Sturz, a prominent social
activist, to start a drug treatment program. They approached me because
I understood how drug treatment fights crime and enhances a community
and because I was a black professional who could talk to street people.

I met with Sturz, who was head of the Vera Institute of Justice, a
private foundation he had founded in 1961 with philanthropist Lou
Schweitzer to reform the criminal justice system. Through his work with
Vera, Sturz had learned that crime and drugs were intertwined and that
those involved, as he said in the *New York Times*, were "badly troubled,
with self-destructive drives."

I was offered the directorship of a clinic in Brooklyn with a staff and
a yearly salary of $34,000. When I turned it down, Stutz offered $40,000.
That amounted to twice my take-home pay at the time, and I began to

give it some thought. Interfaith was on the verge of financial collapse, and conditions in New York City's hospitals and drug programs were deplorable.

"Drugs and crime were exploding all around us when John Lindsay became mayor in 1966," recalls Lindsay's former top aide Jay Kriegel. In fact, New York City was ground zero for drug abuse in the United States. The middle class was fleeing the city, and those who remained were up in arms. As Mayor Lindsay approached reelection in the fall of 1969 with an eye on the presidency, he wanted to demonstrate that he was taking action to combat addiction and its social effects. A renowned innovator of social programs, Herb Sturz had close ties to Lindsay. He and other Lindsay supporters wanted to shore the mayor up by launching drug treatment in Brooklyn, then in East New York, and finally in Harlem.

Lindsay abandoned the increasingly discredited Rockefeller-era program described as "civil commitment" that had mandated confinement for addicts and was really an imprisonment of innocent people. He appointed Dr. Ephraim Ramirez as commissioner of the newly created Addiction Services Agency, which favored (over medication) group-based therapeutic communities, where clients were active participants in their own and each other's treatment. Ramirez had initiated such efforts in Puerto Rico. During the Lindsay years, similar centers opened in New York, including Daytop Village (1966), led by Father William B. O'Brien; Odyssey House (1967), founded by Dr. Judianne Densen Gerber; and Phoenix House (1967), founded by Dr. Mitchell S. Rosenthal.

Despite its advantages, becoming drug free in a therapeutic community is a long, slow process. In the mid-1960s those treating drug addiction had begun experimenting with methadone, a synthetic narcotic. Initially, this was perceived by some, notably in the black and Hispanic communities, as replacing one addiction with another. Those administering the programs were called "pushers in white coats."

Still, by the time of the mayoral election, attitudes had shifted. By the end of 1968, Ramirez was no longer with the Addiction Services Agency. A Committee for Expanded Methadone Treatment was established by leading members of the minority community and "good government" individuals, including heavyweights such as Roy Innis, associate national director of the Congress of Racial Equality; Congressman Herman Badillo; State Senator Basil Paterson; and Manhattan Borough President Percy Sutton.

On the other hand, the mayor's support of methadone treatment was opposed by his top-level administrators. Both the Health Services administrator and the commissioner of the Addiction Services Agency rejected introducing methadone maintenance at their respective agencies. So instead of forcing unwilling city agencies to comply, Lindsay asked the Vera Institute of Justice to develop a methadone program that would be city-sponsored but independently operated.

In 1969, when Sturz approached me, I was in favor of using methadone on a short-term basis (a month or so) for detoxification but was unalterably opposed to long-term methadone maintenance. (My view was to change dramatically in time.) Uncertainty about methadone's effectiveness stemmed from a lack of understanding of the neurophysiology of addiction. While considering Vera's offer, I decided to visit the U.S. Public Health Services Hospital, the so-called Narcotic Farm in Lexington, Kentucky, to learn what I could about drug abuse treatment and research.

It's important here to provide some background. The federal government first became involved in the treatment of drug addiction in 1929, when it approved the creation of facilities in Fort Worth, Texas, and Lexington, Kentucky. A combination federal prison, drug treatment hospital, research laboratory, and working farm, the Lexington site opened in 1935 under the name United States Narcotic Farm. (It changed its name a year later to the U.S. Public Health Service Hospital and again in 1967 to the National Institute of Mental Health, Clinical Research Center.) Despite this significant step to address drug abuse, the American mental health establishment overall took the position that addiction, including alcoholism, represented a moral failing and that devoting resources to treatment was wasteful and misguided. Most hospitals might have been expected to throw an alcoholic out on the street.

The term addict was defined by the government as a person who habitually used a habit-forming narcotic drug, thereby endangering public morals, health, safety, and welfare, or as someone who has lost self-control. That addiction was a disease was clear to only a small number of devoted professionals.

"From its opening in 1935, the Narcotic Farm epitomized the nation's ambivalence about how to deal with drug addiction," writes Nancy Campbell, JP Olsen, and Luke Walden in *The Narcotic Farm*. "On the one hand, it functioned as a compassionate and humane hospital," an asylum on a hill surrounded by one thousand acres of farmland where patients could recover from their drug habits. "On the other hand, it was an imposing prison built to incarcerate drug addicts." Originally a federal prison where addicts were transferred for treatment, the farm later admitted volunteers who sought treatment. (Such patients at Lexington have come to be described by at least one prominent researcher as "guinea pigs.")

The Lexington facility had a far-reaching influence. Pioneering practitioners, including Dr. Herbert Kleber and Dr. Jerome Jaffe, spent time there studying its research and treatment methods. For almost forty years, the institution was the main center for drug addiction treatment in the United States. At its height, the facility housed about fifteen hundred patients, of which about a third had volunteered for treatment, while the remaining two-thirds were prisoners. For its time, Lexington was surprisingly progressive, offering individual and group therapies, job training, psychiatric analysis, medical treatment, Alcoholics Anonymous meetings, art, music therapy, and even hydrotherapy with flow baths to soothe the nerves. Patients in Lexington included actor Peter Lorre and beat generation writer William S. Burroughs, who told of his experiences in his novel *Junkie*. "Some of the musicians that came through there, Chet Baker, Sonny Rollins, Howard McGhee...were playing in bands at the Narcotic Farm," said JP Olsen, who made a documentary film about the farm, in an interview on NPR. "Harry Anslinger, who was the famous, and to many notorious, head of narcotic control in the 1940s and '50s, remarked once that the best jazz band in the world was in Lexington. Many people whom I spoke with who were musicians during the '40s and the '50s tell me that it wasn't just dozens of great jazz musicians but literally hundreds of great jazz musicians." Despite its talented clientele, the facility still retained characteristics of a prison with barred windows, though with otherwise modest security.

The main reason for my stay was to study the use of methadone. The substance, which became the most widely used medication for opioid addiction, was first synthesized in 1937 by two German scientists, Gustav Ehrhart and Max Bockmühl, working for the Hoechst laboratory. It was meant to replace morphine, though it's believed that it was never actually tested or used on humans by the Germans. In 1946, methadone found its way into the United States, and in 1948 the Eli Lily Company began manufacturing it here.

A synthetic narcotic, methadone is an odorless, white powder, tablet, or liquid that dissolves easily in water. Synthetic narcotics (opioids), like the naturally occurring opiates (opium and morphine) derived from the seeds of the Asian poppy, work by mimicking the action of the body's naturally occurring pain-reducing chemicals called endorphins and enkephalins. These are found in the brain and spinal cord and reduce pain by combining with opioid receptors (nerves within the central nervous system). Opioids, however, also produce feelings of euphoria as well as hallucinations and can be both physically and psychologically addictive. Though longer acting than heroin, methadone produces the same sort of pain-reducing, sedative effects. Its slow onset, in dramatic contrast to heroin's spiky highs, eliminates mood swings, making an addict feel normal again.

Because of its similarity to heroin, methadone was initially used in government hospitals in the early 1950s for detoxification—a procedure in which progressively decreasing dosages are given until the patient is drug free. A "maintenance dose" of methadone taken orally, usually a Dixie cup-sized mixture of methadone and orange juice, can stabilize patients by mitigating heroin withdrawal symptoms and by lowering the risk of overdose by increasing tolerance. Many street addicts also use cocaine, but there methadone has no effect.

In addition to studying the programs at Lexington in my research on drug treatment, I also contacted Dr. Jerome Jaffe, who in 1967 had set up the Illinois Drug Abuse Program, a complex drug treatment program and therapeutic community under the state's Department of Mental Health. While serving as director, Jaffe conducted significant research on methadone maintenance and became almost unique among treatment providers in his conviction that addiction treatment should include detoxification, therapeutic communities, methadone programs, and outpatient counseling. A committee within the office of Governor Otto Kerner asked him to write a proposal for treating addiction. Not long after, Jaffe became head of the first program in Illinois.

I spent a fruitful two weeks in Chicago with Dr. Jaffe and his colleague Dr. Edward Senay (a paratrooper who had served in the Second World War), two among the handful of pioneers who created modern addiction treatment. Both became lifelong friends from whom I learned a great deal. Dr. Senay, later a professor emeritus of psychiatry at the University of Chicago, recalled: "We had no beginning template. Let me give you a dramatic illustration of this. We admitted a twenty-six-year-old female patient who was six months pregnant and was shooting $500 of heroin a day. Her boyfriend was a high-level dealer, so she could get any amount of heroin she wanted...After I had finished my workup, I said, 'Could you hang around for about thirty minutes? I want to talk to a colleague of mine about your problem' [how to be detoxed without losing the baby]...I went over to see Dr. Jaffe, explained the circumstances, and said, 'What do I do?'

"'I don't know,' he said. 'I don't know of any literature on this.'

"He gave me a list of prominent big-city hospitals in the country to call, and I did. None of them knew what to do with a heroin-addicted woman who was coming into the hospital to deliver a baby. That's where we were. We had to learn that you can't detox pregnant women without a risk of losing the fetus, and we almost lost some of the women."

So, though little was known in the late 1960s and early 1970s about treating addicts, it was a thrilling time to enter the field. Robert DuPont (the first director of the National Institute on Drug Abuse and the second White House drug czar from 1973 to 1977) recalled that the group of people who were then young—myself; Senay; Jaffe, the first drug czar in 1971 under President Nixon; Dupont himself; Herbert Kleber, who founded the Drug Dependence Unit at Yale University, was deputy director at the Office of National Drug Control Policy under George H. W. Bush, and founded the Division on Substance Abuse at Columbia University; and Peter Bourne, drug czar under President Carter—all "had a sense of innovation, a sense of dynamism. A whole new generation, who had not previously been co-opted by the 'civil commitment' idea prominent under Rockefeller, invented the modern treatment programs in the country. What's striking to me is how different it is today. The drug field is no longer populated by innovators who are coming up with new ideas. It has become pretty bureaucratic and pretty static in a lot of ways."

In those innovative days, treatment was more an art requiring intuition than a science, and Drs. Senay and Jaffe convinced me that effective outcomes required a blend of treatment modalities. More confident about my knowledge and understanding of methadone and substance abuse treatment after my trips to Lexington and Chicago, I called Herb Sturz when I returned to New York and accepted the leadership of the Addiction Research and Treatment Corporation (ARTC).

Despite the important work of the people and institutions in Kentucky and Illinois, by the mid 1960s New York was the mecca in drug treatment, though a mecca fraught with disagreement. For many years, the groundbreaking scientists Drs. Vincent Dole and Marie Nyswander controlled the mecca. Vincent Paul Dole Jr. had been born in Chicago and received an MD from Harvard in 1939. Following an internship at Massachusetts General Hospital, he was invited in 1941 to join the Rockefeller Institute for Medical Research in New York. (It became the Rockefeller University in 1965.) During World War II, he served as a lieutenant commander with the Naval Medical Research Unit at the Rockefeller Institute. After the war, he returned to Rockefeller to establish his own laboratory devoted to the study of hypertension. In 1963, Dole turned his attention to the growing epidemic of drug addiction in New York City, a crisis that was being ignored in the world of established medicine. He rejected the notion that addiction was a form of moral weakness and psychopathology and persuaded Rockefeller University President Detlev Bronk to establish the world's first research program on addiction at their hospital. This required permission from the justice system to treat addicts with long criminal records by administering opioid drugs to them without legal interference.

Dole had been influenced by the work of psychiatrist Marie Nyswander and her book *The Drug Addict as Patient*. Nyswander had trained as a physician and surgeon at the Cornell University Medical College. After finishing her studies at Cornell in 1944, she attempted to join the navy but was turned down because women were not accepted as surgeons. She then took a position at the hospital in Lexington (the Narcotic Farm), where she was first exposed to the treatment then given to addicts. In 1955, Nyswander founded the Narcotic Addiction Research Project in New York City, a program for treating addicts using psychotherapy. Through the 1950s and 1960s, she continued to treat addicts in two programs: a clinic for jazz musicians and a local church program. Twenty years of experience proved to her that conventional psychotherapy, detoxification, and lock-up programs for chronic narcotic users failed, not through lack of motivation on the addict's part but for want of effective medical treatment. In 1963, Dole invited Nyswander to join him in his initial efforts to develop a pharmacological therapy for opiate addiction. He also recruited Dr. Mary Jeanne Kreek, a young resident at the Cornell University Medical College, who has continued to work at Rockefeller to this day as an eminent laboratory director and professor. And he brought in Dr. Joyce Lowinson, who helped set up the first inpatient methadone treatment unit at Beth Israel Hospital and later became professor of psychiatry and executive director of the Division of Substance Abuse at the Albert Einstein College of Medicine.

In early 1964, the team began the clinical research work at Rockefeller University that provided the first scientific foundation for methadone treatment. They admitted to the hospital a group of fewer than twenty, tough, hard-core addicts who had used heroin for at least fourteen years and had been in and out of detoxification centers (in many cases, in and out of prison) over the past decade. Instead of administering a set dose of methadone over a period of time, they actually increased the amount until an addict was stabilized on a higher daily dose of methadone than he had previously used of heroin. They argued that maintaining addicts on high doses, from fifty to eighty milligrams, established a pharmacological block that negated a benefit from heroin, thereby discouraging its use. They also claimed that since addicts received their methadone free, they had no reason to turn to crime. After several months, Dole and Nyswander reached the then groundbreaking conclusion that addiction was a disease of the brain rather than an act of either criminal behavior or weak character, and that restoring an addict's neurochemical balance, thus abolishing the craving for narcotics, must precede social rehabilitation. (As is now widely known, recent brain imaging and genetics research shows a strong biological basis for addiction.)

Their goal was to return the addict to the community as a functioning, useful member of society. In May 1965, Dole and Nyswander published their findings in the prestigious *Journal of the American Medical Association*. In a related article in 1966, Dole, Nyswander, and Kreek concluded: "A stable blockade against the narcotic effects of heroin can be maintained by a single daily oral dose of methadone. Blockade is established by a gradual increase in dosage to a stabilization level; thereafter the dose of methadone remains constant...With the maintenance treatment the patients have lost their craving for heroin. No patient has become readdicted to heroin."

Their results had an immediate impact, followed by an increase in funding and support for Dole's programs. After the initial studies conducted by Drs. Dole and Nyswander, Dr. Mathilde Krim, then a researcher at the Memorial Sloan Kettering Cancer Center and later a leader in the fight against AIDS, had meetings at her home in Manhattan where she invited public and private individuals to support their work.

Within a year of his initial findings, Dole expanded his small clinical study to a program at the Beth Israel Medical center (formerly Manhattan General Hospital), where in 1965 Dr. Joyce Lowinson, working with Dr. Harold Trigg, opened the first inpatient ward. It was soon followed by a ward for female patients under the directorship of Dr. Melissa Freeman, and then by an outpatient clinic. With a two-year waiting list, Beth Israel also established a small satellite unit of six beds at Harlem Hospital under Dr. James Robinson and administered a number of other methadone clinics throughout the city.

In their prime, Dole and Nyswander had already become iconic figures in the history of drug abuse treatment. At the same time, they were in the community but not of the community. Beth Israel was a dominant provider of methadone treatment in New York, and Dole and Nyswander's programs were located primarily in midtown Manhattan, far from the looming problems elsewhere in the city. In contrast, Lindsay and Sturz advocated treating addicts in their own communities, putting them at odds with Dole and Nyswander. In May 1969, Dole wrote a letter to Herbert Sturz criticizing his proposed program: "It is a medically naïve, unworkable mess—in my opinion...The administrative and clinical personnel that would be needed to operate such a program do not exist, at any salary, apart from the personnel that we have trained...You have a ten ton airplane with a one horsepower motor."

As late as the summer of 2012, four decades after I began the Addiction Research and Treatment Corporation, Herman Joseph, who had worked as an investigator at Rockefeller University for Dr. Dole and coauthored articles with him, recalled how strongly opposed Dole was at first to me and my work. We were, after all, in competition with Dole for public funds, and our approaches were markedly different. We were experimenting with lower doses of methadone than Dole would ever consider.

Referring first to the Vera Institute and then to ARTC, Joseph commented: "These schmucks had the chutzpah to question Dole's metabolic theory. That led to the split between Dole and ARTC. Fifty milligrams was the highest dose they were going to give. There was a corresponding pressure to accept further downward shifts. When he learned this, Dole hit the ceiling. ARTC didn't know what they were doing. They literally did not understand what addiction was, what heroin was, why methadone was being used."

Of course, after a short time, I accepted the evidence established by Dole, Nyswander, and others that higher doses were sometimes needed. Dole and Nyswander were skeptical of me as well because I had spoken out against aspects of their approach. First, the inpatient approach that limited the number of addicts treated in a given period of time, despite certain advantages, was wrong, I believed, for the black and minority community where the numbers were enormous. In addition, I had stated that it was unfair to expect Harlem residents to travel downtown to Beth Israel, adding that methadone providers failed to focus enough on minorities and the minority culture. Their hostility toward me persisted for over a decade until Dole came to see my work and witness firsthand my compassion for patients. (In 1992, I received the Nyswander-Dole "Marie" Award given by the American Association for the Treatment of Opioid Dependence.)

Despite disagreements within Lindsay's administration as to the effectiveness of methadone, the mayor concluded that methadone clinics were the most effective way to treat large numbers of addicts. "Real expansion was the perceived need and our goal," Kriegel said. "Our objective was to find a way to test on a large scale if methadone could be effective and carefully controlled in an ambulatory treatment program, which could be expanded rapidly, at low cost, without the enormous demands for hospital-based space.

"But Dole and Nyswander were adamant that everything be controlled by them and done their way. Their rigid approach insisted on inpatient treatment, which was slow and costly to expand."

Sturz, who had a number of meetings with Dole and Nyswander at the time, recalled: "The patients they worked with at first were all inpatients at the Beth Israel Medical Center. It was very small, ten or twelve patients. I told the Doles that we wanted to help seventy or ninety patients. Dole and Nyswander thought that they couldn't handle that. I just made up the number seventy, but we had many thousands in mind. The Doles were very upset about that [number], and they were the only game in town for methadone."

Despite Lindsay's support, some of his staff were concerned about the sponsorship and management of our planned clinic. Mitchell Ginsberg (the administrator of the New York City's Human Resources Administration) and Bernard Bucove (the Health Services Administrator) wrote a memo in March 1969 to the mayor: "We are in complete agreement on the desirability and necessity of expanding the Methadone program but feel that the proposal submitted by the Vera Foundation will not accomplish this objective...Furthermore, we believe that the sponsorship of this program by Vera or any outside organization would lead to further serious fragmentation of services of this nature."

A few weeks later, while on vacation in Cozumel, Mexico, Sturz received a call from Kriegel saying that the Lindsay administration wanted to go ahead with an experimental methadone program but had concerns about how it would be managed. Kriegel asked Sturz if he would be willing to set up a nonprofit organization under the auspices of the Vera Institute of Justice to bypass the bureaucratic and financial hurdles of the New York City government. To accomplish this, federal or private funds would be needed. Sturz, recalling it all enthusiastically forty-five years later, said, "At the time, my sense was: you try whatever is promising; you measure it; you evaluate it; you put controls on it. That was my approach. Though I had created not-for-profits, we had to figure out a protocol. Where would you locate it? Who would take responsibility?"

Sturz moved quickly to get approval from his Vera board and offered his friend Nicholas deB. Katzenbach the chairmanship of the new clinic's board. Katznebach had served as attorney general under President Lyndon Johnson and then as an IBM vice president. (IBM later helped establish the clinic with financial aid and computers.). Katzenbach, in turn, brought to the board his old friend Burke Marshall, who had served with him at the Justice Department. Other members included Brooklyn District Attorney Eugene Gold and Justice Edward R. Dudley of the New York State Supreme Court. It was a star-studded group.

"Herb and I had a meeting and talked about who should be in charge," Katzenbach said at his home in Princeton, New Jersey, a few months before he died. He recalled interviewing me at his home in Riverdale. "After that," he said, "there was a meeting in Brooklyn with a bunch of people from the neighborhood, and it was a pretty nasty meeting. They saw methadone as a way of whites keeping control over blacks, and they got pretty nasty with Herb and me," adding that "[Primm] was there and calmed them down. It wasn't fun to be attacked by a group of people you are trying to help."

Chapter Three

Persistence

I ran and ran and ran every day, and I acquired this sense of
determination, this sense of spirit that I would never,
never give up, no matter what else happened.

Wilma Rudolph, Olympic track star

On October 8, 1969, a month before Lindsay's reelection, the
Addiction Research and Treatment Center (ARTC) opened its doors
at 937 Fulton Street in the Bedford-Stuyvesant area of Brooklyn, in an old
Salvation Army building that had previously been an alcoholism treatment center for men. The weekend before we opened, Katzenbach and
Sturz joined me and volunteer staff to paint where needed in the four-
story building. ("And I'm not a very good painter," Katzenbach remi-
nisced.) At the dedication, Mayor Lindsay described the project as "the
largest methadone program ever undertaken in the nation." It was also
the first black-managed methadone treatment program in the country
and would go on to become the oldest and largest minority-operated, not-
for-profit drug treatment program in the United States.

But as we opened our actual doors to treat addicts, many doors of
public opinion and community support were slammed in our faces, leaving me frustrated and often angry about the constant criticism. The fact
was that working against drug abuse entailed involvement in the entire
dysfunctional social reality of the addict and the surrounding community,

situated in the complex context of New York City. You couldn't tease out addiction from the big picture; the whole mess came at you.

Brooklyn had been chosen as the site for ARTC because Lindsay believed that a drug abuse center should be an integral part of the Model Cities Program (part of Lyndon Johnson's Great Society and War on Poverty), and he was close to Horace Morancie, director of the Central Brooklyn Model Cities Program, and to Model Cities Administrator J. B. Williams. In the beginning, Brooklyn was very rough, and the attitude of the black and minority community was absolutely hostile. Everybody, it seemed, had his or her territory, so determining who ran a community organization and working through that person to influence the larger group was tricky. "It was a very turbulent time," recalls Danny Cook, who had worked at Interfaith with me and became one of ARTC's first employees as a counselor. "Black militancy and skepticism of the power structure were very high. There was an explosion of drugs.

"When I was a kid, the people who used heroin were hustlers, pimps, and musicians, but it was not an everyday thing for guys in the street. Then it became just that. And with no means to support their habit, these people became criminals.

"Some of my best friends were addicts; one was closer to me than my brother. He got a job working for the post office in the sixties, then got married and was doing okay. He was smoking a little weed. But then he got busted and lost his post office job. Last time I saw his face, it was on a poster on the wall at the health department. He was all strung out. I suppose he died in the streets. I knew about drugs and what they did. When this boy lost the post office job, he had to sell reefers on the side. Then he started selling heroin, and he went down and his brother went with him. Mostly people were dealing marijuana. Among addicts there were three distinct groups: black, white, and Puerto Rican. The black addict used heroin; spending ten to thirty dollars a day, he had to steal. The whites used all manner of prescription drugs they got from physicians, spending five or six dollars a week to stay high. Puerto Ricans used everything. Drugs were everywhere. Harlem was the drug capital of America, and Brooklyn was not far behind."

To complicate matters, although methadone was our best hope when ARTC began, it was badmouthed everywhere. Oddly, street people were aligned with right-wing whites in their solid opposition to any drug treatment facility in their neighborhood; "Not in My Backyard" (NIMBY) was the catch phrase. Black folk considered methadone the white man's drug and said I was selling out as a pawn of the white establishment. Flyers circulated in the neighborhood barbershops and beauty parlors bearing pictures of me in a white doctor's coat with the caption "Pushers Come in All Disguises."

On a cold November day in 1969, about a month after we had opened, four men from Nat's Coming, a black militant organization named after slave-leader Nat Turner, forced their way into our building. Two were brandishing machetes as they barged into my third-floor office threatening my life. "We're going to cut your head off," they taunted. At first, I tried to reason with them. "Let's talk about what we're contributing to the community," I started to explain. But the intruders moved menacingly toward me. Then, drawing on my years growing up on the streets of Harlem and the Bronx and on my military training as a paratrooper, I told them, "If you come in here with your bullshit, you'd better bring your lunch."

The intruders knew immediately that I meant that they'd better be prepared to stay for a long, drawn-out struggle. I told them that I understood their fears and complaints, and I listened to what they had to say. After a while, the men calmed down and, muttering vulgarities, sauntered out of my office without damaging the premises or harming me. But for the next six months, Mayor Lindsay provided me with New York City police officers as bodyguards wherever I went, which surprisingly didn't affect my relationship with the community. Ironically, one of the bodyguards was Colonel Jetty Gates who had been my commander in the 82nd Airborne Division.

The verbal threats lasted for about half a year, but the hostile atmosphere continued longer, and the police often were not much help. When I tried to have a man known as Slim, the biggest drug dealer in Brooklyn, arrested for selling drugs across the street from ARTC, the community who didn't want drug dealers in the neighborhood supported my efforts, but the police wouldn't bust him. I later learned that he was working with the Drug Enforcement Administration (DEA) as an informer.

Soon after we opened, we found ourselves under harsh criticism from both the black and white communities of Fort Greene. The controversy swirling around ARTC wasn't simply in the academy or laboratory, on the street or in the community; it was becoming an object of citywide and potentially national attention. Thus, in June 1970, a year after ARTC was founded, the *New York Times* published a long article by Richard Severo under the headline "Rumor, Intrigue and Criticism Beset City's Brooklyn Methadone Center." Describing the contradictory criticism aimed at us, the *Times* reported that ARTC was accused of both "giving too much drugs and too little, of being harsh with addicts and of overprotecting them, of advocating black militancy and of being the tools of the white power structure and of being conservative, radical, conformist and obstructionist, all at the same time." The article concluded: "What is being thought and said about the program is New York City's addiction treatment picture in microcosm: a sour stew of Byzantine rumor, intrigue and invective sprinkled liberally with defensiveness and personal ambition."

The anonymous sources mentioned to support these claims were most likely familiar critics of our programs: directors of therapeutic, drug-free communities and black militants who regarded methadone as a new means to "shackle blacks."

The article cited criticisms that "club-carrying guards were terrorizing patients," an exaggeration of the fact that security guards, who carried nightsticks, had been hired after I had been threatened by the belligerent Nat's Coming members, and after Conrad Mauge, a top executive at ARTC, had been physically attacked in a parking lot outside one of the centers by black militants. Another claim maintained that methadone was occasionally stolen from the center, but our chief pharmacist is quoted in the article denying that there had been any such thefts. Another complaint was that the center had given methadone to children, but this was absurd. We had very strict rules that patients had to be at least twenty-one years old.

The *Times* also mentioned that about two years before the opening of ARTC, I had publicly characterized methadone as simply another addictive drug. Calling me outspoken and sometimes emotional, the article accurately quoted me as saying, "I'm still skeptical of methadone [for long-term treatment]. I don't buy Dr. Dole's suggestion that this is just like taking insulin. But I think this drug can help a lot of addicts—maybe thousands of them—who just aren't going to make it any other way. And if I think a guy can't make it any other way, I'm going to give him methadone."

Finally, a black militant and former addict told the *Times* that he thought I was no better than a heroin peddler. But within a few hours of the interview, according to the article, this man, a former addict, was on the phone with me making it clear that his words had been misstated, warning that the white power structure was "out to get" me. His behavior was not a sign that I was winning over the black community but rather a play for personal gain; the next day he visited our clinic asking for a job.

The *Times* concluded that ARTC "is a project that has all but been cut off from normal professional contact with other agencies dispensing methadone—trying to establish rapport with the people of Bedford-Stuyvesant while placating or rebuffing critics from outside the community [such as Dole and Nyswander]." Clearly, we were in everyone's crosshairs, from the Dole-Nyswander contingent to the various community constituencies.

Since my overriding goal was to build a working relationship with our local people, and I realized that the Brooklyn community would never accept us or, more specifically, our mission as they understood it, I began in the early seventies to appoint additional local leaders to our board of directors when vacancies occurred and after Katzenbach had left the ARTC board. (Katzenbach later said, "I wanted to get out not only because it was working—in fact it was working fairly well— but because I didn't feel that the board or me or Herb Sturz, for that matter, had any power." He added that I didn't listen to him and did whatever I wanted; that I would "scream, holler, and shout when things weren't working" and then would "calm down and be practical"; and that I "turned out to be a pretty good politician.")

Our board soon included community figures such as Judge J. B. Williams (Mayor Lindsay's Model Cities administrator) and Horace Morancie (of the Model Cities Program in Brooklyn). Other board members important to our success included attorney Arthur N. Brook; physician Juan Bailey; Vivian Bright, business administrator for the Berean Baptist Church; Joyce Hall, executive director of the Federation of County Networks; District Attorney Eugene Gold; Judge Judy Mitchell; Dr. Robert Morgan, Director of the Bowery Project; and later Gwendolyn Towns, an educator and wife of former Congressman Edolphus Towns. Finally, it cannot be overstated how critical it was that Mayor Lindsay was committed to methadone maintenance treatment, describing it as "a breakthrough in the large-scale attack on the plague of narcotics." He was crucial to our early success in securing funding and reaching out to other political leaders, ensuring that politicians like Brooklyn Congresswoman Shirley Chisholm supported us. I met a number of times with Lindsay and well remember his presence at ARTC for a party celebrating his birthday on November 24, 1970.

A year after ARTC opened in Brooklyn, the mayor pushed to open other methadone treatment centers. The ARTC Fort Greene clinic (the original location) was in a neighborhood where, as the *Daily News* reported in 1973, fifty thousand people lived and where there were over three thousand addicts under treatment. About four years after our opening, there were five other, mainly therapeutic, drug treatment centers in addition to our primary clinic as well as a methadone clinic at Cumberland Hospital—all in an area of ten by sixteen blocks. The newspaper called it "the methadone capital of the world."

We adhered to our preferred outpatient approach with admission criteria, unique at the time, to accept the widest possible range of patients, including addicts with a long history of criminal activity, with unsuccessful experiences in other programs, and who were unemployed—basically, a hard-core patient population. "We were providing many more services than any other methadone program," former ARTC Senior Vice President Robert Sage reminded me. "At other programs people simply would get medicated and see their counselors once a month." Our whole approach was based on my philosophy of a "supermarket" of services in which the many needs of drug abuse patients had to be met in addition to dispensing methadone. We provided vocational and medical services and were one of the first programs to offer psychiatric services and group counseling, in which patients met once a week for about an hour with a staff counselor and approximately ten other patients. Such meetings included open discussions in which patients could raise any subject. Our overarching goal was to treat the whole person—to habilitate each individual. Our patients came from such deprived socioeconomic and educational backgrounds that it was a question of starting at base level. I don't think anyone else's goals were as comprehensive as ours in those early days. Such treatment can take many years; there are still patients at our Fort Greene clinic who were with us when it opened forty-five years ago.

In 1975, an outside team was created by the Vera Institute to evaluate ARTC's first few years. James Vorenberg at Harvard studied ARTC's impact on criminality; Herbert Kleber at Yale, the medical impact; and Irving Lukoff at Columbia, the social impact of our work. Their conclusions motivated me and all of ARTC to adopt a course correction on several fronts. In their final report, "Methadone Maintenance—Modest Help for A Few," the outside evaluators noted that fifty-one deaths from heroin overdose had occurred among the patient pool of 1,818 during our first three years. The cause was a drop in methadone level that provoked a craving for heroin, prompting patients to shoot up and die as a result. It was also found that 80 to 90 percent of patients who left methadone treatment after stabilization became heroin users again, leading to my belief in long-term methadone treatment. (Later, in their seminal study of 1991 on the effectiveness of methadone treatment, funded by the National Institute on Drug Abuse, John C. Ball and Alan Ross concluded that heroin addicts who continued with methadone maintenance for a year or longer had a marked decrease in intravenous drug use and criminal acts.)

These were the early days of methadone research and treatment, when we were learning from experience in adjusting doses based on several studies as well as from our own research. Most importantly, we learned from the needs of individual patients. Over time, we became flexible and, following best practices, accepted many of the scientific conclusions of Dole and Nyswander combined with our own.

Chapter Four

Washington

—∞∞∞—

Of all the forms of inequality, injustice in health care is the most shocking and inhumane.

Martin Luther King Jr.

While ARTC was slowly getting off the ground, drug abuse was moving to center stage on the national level. In September 1970, the White House asked my colleague and friend Jerome Jaffe—at whose Chicago clinic I had observed multiple modalities of treatment, including detoxification, drug-free therapy, and methadone maintenance—to assemble a committee to investigate and produce a report on treatment, research, and prevention, with guidelines for the government on funding allocations. As the report was being finalized, a White House staff member asked Jaffe to include a rebuttal to criticism of methadone maintenance made by some federal agencies. The National Institute of Mental Health, for example, had expressed concerns about the long-term psychological effects of methadone, which were then undocumented. The Bureau of Narcotics and Dangerous Drugs feared that methadone from government programs would be sold on the black market, and the American Medical Association doubted the medical effectiveness of the drug. Jaffe's committee report was delivered in December.

Meanwhile, the point men for substance abuse issues at the White House included John Ehrlichman, counsel and assistant to the president for domestic affairs; Egil "Bud" Krogh, who—reporting to Ehrlichman—had never used any drug, not even cigarettes or alcohol; and his young staff assistant Jeff Donfeld. "At a time when his entire generation was tuning in, turning on, and dropping out, Donfeld liked to boast that he had never been intoxicated, even on alcohol," journalist Michael Massing wrote in *The Fix,* a comprehensive look at America's drug war.

As the White House liaison with the District of Columbia, Krogh had been briefed by Robert Dupont, who had worked for the district's department of corrections and then ran the DC Narcotics Treatment Administration. Dupont recommended the "possibilities of using methadone in Washington, DC, based on a 'filling station' principle, in which addicts would have the same easy access to acquiring methadone as motorists have to gasoline." A national methadone program presented a challenge, however, as the administration didn't want to be perceived as sanctioning the use of an addictive and controversial drug.

The president's staff visited many programs; each said theirs was the best. Following his visit to Jaffe's clinic in Chicago, Donfeld described his mixed modality approach as "different strokes for different folks"—which might, he thought, shield the methadone program from political criticism.

Meanwhile, Nixon's aides knew that Lindsay, a possible democratic presidential candidate for 1972, had successfully implemented a methadone program in New York. Though Ehrlichman continued to express doubts about the morality and wisdom of the administration distributing methadone in the ghettos, he was eventually persuaded by Donfeld's assertion that this was the only means of reducing crime before the 1972 election. Action was blocked, however, by Attorney General John Mitchell and Secretary of Health, Education, and Welfare Elliot Richardson, who were not about to let the Nixon administration be open to the charge that it was advocating and granting funds for methadone. This infighting over treatment persisted until the Vietnam War intervened, bringing with it the problem of war-scarred veterans who had turned to drugs.

Nixon was worried about the possibility of hundreds of thousands of heroin-addicted soldiers returning from the battlefield. In May 1971, Republican Congressman Robert Steele of Connecticut and Democrat Morgan Murphy of Illinois released a report about their earlier fact-finding trip to Vietnam. They had disturbing news that fueled Nixon's fears: 10 to 15 percent of US servicemen in Vietnam were actively addicted to heroin. It was clear to Krogh that the sources of supply couldn't be controlled, and White House aides suggested that soldiers in Vietnam be tested for heroin addiction. The military had at first ignored then decided to prosecute heroin use by troops. Even an amnesty program failed to solve the problem, prompting Congress to earmark $10 million to the Veterans Administration to combat drug abuse and $160 million to the National Institute of Mental Health for community-based drug addiction clinics. While some authorities recommended methadone and others therapeutic communities, the military recoiled: "Get the hell out of our units. Leave us alone."

At the end of May, Jaffe was called to the White House, where plans were discussed for setting up a special office on drug abuse. Shortly after, he had a meeting at the Pentagon, where he told a group of generals about a new machine that could detect drug use in urine. At first the generals balked at the complexity suggested. Not intimidated by all the brass sitting in front of him, Jaffe broke the ice: "I cannot believe that the mightiest army on earth can't get its troops to piss in a bottle. Gentlemen, the White House wants something done about this sooner rather than later." The generals left the room briefly and, when they returned, pledged cooperation.

In a logical move for a law-and-order president, Nixon reasoned that drugs were closely related to crime—his main political issue. Thus, on June 17, 1971, the president announced that "America's public enemy number one in the United States is drug abuse. In order to fight and defeat this enemy, it is necessary to wage a new, all-out offensive." Treatment instead of law enforcement would be the centerpiece of this initiative and would receive most of the attention and funding. On the same day, June 17, a date the Pentagon had set for having a urine-testing program up and running in Vietnam, Nixon formally introduced the Special Action Office for Drug Abuse Prevention (SAODAP), naming Jerome Jaffe, a young, democratic psychiatrist, as the nation's first "drug czar."

"The president called me into his cabinet room," Jaffe remembered. "There was a whole bunch of congressmen and senators there, and he said that he was going to announce a major initiative on drug abuse." Jaffe later learned that in the various drafts of Nixon's speech, the writers had estimated the number of addicts in America at 300,000 and the cost of crime attributed to heroin addiction at $10 billion per year. But as memos and drafts piled up, it became clear that such facts were elusive. Estimates varied between 250,000 and 600,000 addicts— but without consensus. In addition, the administration and its speechwriters, while trumpeting the president's bold initiative, wanted to keep a morally safe distance from what was still viewed as depravity. They certainly wanted to avoid the implication that a drug epidemic had begun or flourished under Nixon's watch. "During his speech," Jaffe continued, "Nixon pointed to me and said, 'Dr. Jaffe is going over to Vietnam.' With no preparation, not even a change of clothes, I had to go in front of the press corps."

Krogh later recalled, "The president basically said to Jaffe, 'Go out there, and if you need to kick some tail, you do it.'"

Following Congressmen Steele and Murphy's report on heroin addiction on the battlefield in Southeast Asia, Nixon's war on drugs in America was reoriented to distant Vietnam. Jaffe's brief was to travel there without delay. In short order, I received an urgent phone call: "Dr. Jaffe wants to see you immediately." I rushed to return the call. "Beny, I want you to go to Vietnam in a week with me," he said. Jaffe believed my knowledge and experience of the military could strengthen and lend credibility to the effort. Needless to say, his appointment and his choice of me as an assistant changed my life, catapulting me from Harlem and Brooklyn to Washington and Vietnam. The White House knew of my work, and because there were many black soldiers in Vietnam, it wanted some color. The fact is, too, that I was one of the few black practicing experts in the country on drug abuse treatment. Still, I'm not entirely sure what Nixon's mission was at that point. In part, he sent us to Vietnam to appear proactive. As I had discovered at ARTC, and as Jaffe knew well, tackling large-scale abuse treatment, and now in a war zone, was guaranteed to be a trial and error process. But it was critical to begin.

I hesitated. My wife, Delphine, had recently been diagnosed with breast cancer; understandably, she wanted me to stay home. The White House was persistent: "We'll take care of her and put you up in Washington, where you can stay for a few days with your wife; then we'll fly you to New York and let her off and then fly you to Alaska, Hong Kong, and Vietnam." And so we worked it out.

There were suggestions in Congress for civilly committing all soldiers who tested positive. The idea of a steady stream of heroin addicts trained in combat returning daily from Vietnam made Congress very uncomfortable. The administration's plan was that we would test every soldier up to the rank of major. Those who had remained heroin-free would board a plane; the others would be guests of the military in Vietnam for brief treatment.

To the military brass, this approach seemed soft and contrary to the then Code of Military Justice that categorized heroin use as a court-martial offense. So, to clear the way for a program of universal testing, the president simply ordered the necessary change in the Code of Military Justice. In addition, the government later reversed some of the bad conduct and dishonorable discharges people had received simply as a result of drug use. The program had checks to identify urine samples and to confirm positive results with gas chromatography, a technique that measures various compounds in a sample.

The logistics of the program were mind-boggling, yet it was up and running in two weeks. The military built facilities for urine collection, and new discoveries made it feasible to test roughly one thousand people daily. The immediate effect was that, as soldiers learned that heroin could be detected, its use diminished. Word spread quickly that only in cases of deep addiction were test results positive. Some hadn't heard about the testing, but they seemed to be exceedingly few. Our testing process demonstrated that, though heroin remained available and cheap, intervention could quickly reduce its use. To administer treatment, the military constructed detoxification facilities in Vietnam.

Jaffe and I flew there on July 5 and returned on July 13, whereupon we went to the Western White House at San Clemente to report to the president, who was clearly pleased to hear that fewer than 15 percent of the troops were positive.

After an hour or more on the patio, he walked with us to our car, which surprised me. Nixon was always receptive to me, later inviting my wife and me to the White House. I felt honored, of course, and was bitterly disappointed when some of the Nixon tapes released later revealed prejudice toward blacks, Jews, and other minorities. Until then, I had only positive feelings about him.

After our meeting with the president, we met with Ehrlichman, Krogh, and Donfeld to report on our trip. On the way to the airport, Krogh explained that he had just been given a new assignment by Nixon that would consume most of his time. I learned later that the assignment eventually led to the "White House Plumbers" unit responsible for the break-in at Daniel Ellsberg's psychiatrist's office in California, a breach that famously became part of the Watergate scandal.

I don't think any of us in the Special Action Office were wedded to any particular political party or philosophy. We focused entirely on running drug treatment programs, and I thought the government's war on drugs—a first—was a good thing.

Following our meeting at San Clemente, Jaffe asked me to return to DC and work as an advisor in the Special Action Office. Robert Dupont, who followed as the second drug czar, quipped that I was "kind of an alter ego to Jaffe." From then on, I commuted almost weekly between my offices at ARTC in Brooklyn and in Washington, where I was at my desk by 9:00 a.m. (During that period, I was also an adjunct professor at the Hunter College School of Social Work and at the M.J. Lewi College of Podiatry in Harlem.)

Immediately, Jaffe and I created a program that sent drug abuse counselors, mainly from Jaffe's Chicago program and mine in New York, to Veterans Administration hospitals and army posts to give instruction on treating returning veterans who were still abusing drugs. Our personnel fanned out across the country to establish procedures. We taught people how to treat withdrawal symptoms and follow up with therapeutic communities. There was no recommendation for methadone use at that time; we thought that therapeutic communities were sufficient.

Meanwhile, an advisory committee was created for the administration's public relations anti-heroin crusade. Among those chosen was Sammy Davis Jr., who was known to be concerned about the fate of black colleges. Nixon personally assured him that "the administration is behind black colleges and has thus far given more than $150 million to them." Several months later, Davis traveled to Vietnam, though a planned television program featuring Davis and Nixon failed to be produced after two firms that had expressed interest, the Hoffmann-La Roche pharmaceutical company and the Hughes Sports Network, neglected to provide the necessary funds. Others selected to be on the committee included Gayle Sayers, the football star, and television and radio personality Art Linkletter. (Linkletter's daughter Diane had committed suicide in 1969, which her father attributed to drug use.)

Among the many trips I took as part of the new initiative was a journey to San Antonio, Texas, to explain treatment protocols to professionals caring for veterans returning from Vietnam. While there, sudden pains in my chest convinced me I was having a heart attack. The Nixon White House called President Johnson's physician, who traveled to treat me at the Brooke General Hospital at Fort Sam Houston in San Antonio, where I stayed for about a week. It was determined that the pain was stress related, and I was advised to slow down, which I did do—for a few months.

One of the most important consequences of the Vietnam initiative was to characterize addicts as patients who needed treatment rather than as second-class citizens, the dregs of the earth. For the first time, the federal government was making a commitment to treatment in the community. I don't think it would have been possible without the sense of urgency that came from the heroin use in Vietnam. It was easy to stigmatize and marginalize heroin users in the inner cities, to treat them as law enforcement problems. It's more complicated when they're veterans.

In April 1973, the results of a $400,000 study of drug addiction among Vietnam veterans sponsored by the Special Action Office and conducted by Dr. Lee Robins, a sociologist at Washington University in St. Louis, were released. The study was to determine the prevalence of opiate use and addiction among servicemen returning from Vietnam and to discover how many continued their use once they returned to the states.

At a news conference, which first publicized the report, Richard S. Wilbur, assistant secretary of defense (health and environment) in the Pentagon, said, "Who could have predicted two years ago that almost all drug abusers and drug dependents [from Vietnam] could have been restored to a drug-free existence in our society?" Dr. Robins, however, was displeased: first, that the Pentagon, rather than the White House drug abuse office or another nonmilitary representative, had released her findings; and second, that Dr. Wilbur had, she claimed, "oversimplified" her findings concerning drug use by Vietnam veterans. What she had written was that, while drug use in Vietnam was "quite high," the use by returning servicemen was "shockingly low, considering levels of wartime use." Her study concluded that "although nearly half the men addicted in Vietnam tried narcotics again after their return, only six percent overall got re-addicted...We found little to justify the view of heroin as an especially dangerous drug."

This, of course, flew in the face of everything known about heroin and drug addiction generally. People thought that somehow she was lying, or did something wrong, or was politically influenced. She spent years trying to defend the integrity of the study. But over forty years later, the findings of Robins's study are widely accepted.

Jerome Jaffe later stated that he believed that about 5 percent of returning Vietnam veterans relapsed to heroin use in the first year. Clearly, the contrast between the war environment and that of normal life in the United States was key. When addicts in the United States returned to their homes in the inner cities following treatment, relapse rates hovered around 90 percent, undoubtedly due to the social and economic stresses of that environment.

At the time of President Nixon's landslide reelection of 1972, I was still engaged with the Special Action Office. Nevertheless, members of the president's staff asked if I would be interested in becoming ambassador to Haiti, potentially a worthwhile assignment. But it was not a good time to be away. My wife was still undergoing treatment for cancer, and I declined the offer.

Also, while busy with federally based projects as a presidential advisor, I remained keenly aware of conditions in New York City. One day in the fall of 1972, I was having lunch in the White House mess at a table with a number of people I didn't know. They were discussing roads and bridges, public works improvement projects in the poor, coal-mining areas of Appalachia.

"Appalachia?" I interrupted, "I grew up in the heart of Appalachia in West Virginia. But in New York, where I live now, the people desperately need help. You need to focus on the cities also." The man to whom I had addressed these words turned and said, "Doctor, that's interesting." I later learned that he was Secretary of Commerce Maurice Stans.

A month later, I got a call from John Ehrlichman saying that he and Krogh wanted to meet with me in New York. We had breakfast at the Plaza Hotel, where they asked if I would be willing to support New York Congressman John Rooney, a conservative Democrat and chairman of the House Armed Services Committee, who was running in a primary against Allard Lowenstein, a liberal former Congressman. They said, "We think Rooney will lose, but the president wants him reelected. We want you to come out for Rooney. In return, we will give you public works improvement project grants of $1.2 million a year for the next ten years. There will be a news conference, and we want you to announce this program for Rooney's district. He will be there." Rooney knew me. He represented the district in Brooklyn where both ARTC's headquarters on Chapel Street and our original clinic on Fulton Street were located. Ehrlichman said Secretary Stans had repeated my comments urging public works grants in New York that would enable people to obtain training and jobs. I told Ehrlichman, "I'd be more than happy to do it."

"By the way, Doctor, how are you registered?" Ehrlichman asked as we were leaving.

"I'm a retired army officer," I said.

"No, no, not the draft, I'm not talking about that. How are you registered to vote?"

"I'm an independent."

"An independent? I think the president would prefer you be a Republican. He is getting ready to appoint you to a couple of advisory committees, and it would look better if you were a Republican."

Despite some misgivings, I changed my registration that day from Independent to Republican. Putting a firm foundation under ARTC was more important to me than a political party or ideology.

At the Rooney press conference, Gabe Pressman, a reporter from WNBC-TV, questioned the Congressman's commitment to diversity. Supportive of my work, Pressman asked, "Dr. Primm, you've been a very responsible revolutionary; you've done things that are very constructive. Why are you supporting Congressman Rooney, who has never had a black or Hispanic on his staff?"

"Here is a man who is ready to act on behalf of the African American and Hispanic communities," I answered. "He is helping to provide a public works improvement grant. We will start vocational training for people who are out of work, to help them find jobs at the Brooklyn Navy Yard. How in the world could I not be for him? And how in the world could our community not be for him?" After a pause, I said, "The Lord works in mysterious ways."

Rooney won reelection. The president was happy, and ARTC received $1.2 million per year for ten years. The federal grant helped to fund a range of social services, primarily a skills center for job training. Unfortunately, at the end of ten years (1983), we had to close the center and discontinue the legal, vocational, and educational services that had been funded under the federal grant. The building remained our property, and an ARTC clinic (now known as START) is there today. Thereafter, we looked for innovative ways to provide approximately the same programs and services with less money but were unsuccessful.

Chapter Five

Maelstrom

Keep the faith, baby!

Adam Clayton Powell Jr.

D espite the Nixon administration's generous funding and my ongoing efforts at ARTC, the decade of the 70s was marked by ceaseless strife. In October 1973, the *Times* published another article about us. "There has been constant harassment," I told reporter David C. Berliner in exasperation, "and I and my whole staff are just about ready to hand the community the methadone, hand the community the patients and say, 'You treat them.' Our program has constant evaluation and constant monitoring from government agencies, and if this kind of program has to suffer these kinds of attacks, then, my God, what will happen to all the little programs?"

A major source of antagonism with the Brooklyn community was loitering, a problem so great that a state law was passed to control it. A year after opening, we had over one thousand patients at the Fort Greene clinic. The patients would congregate on the sidewalk in front of the building, and the neighbors were incensed. And on this question, they were right. Community opposition mostly stemmed from a concern for stability and quality of life in the streets.

At the beginning, there was no limit on the total number of patients who could be served by the clinic. But soon the maximum allowed under law was reduced to five hundred, a decision likely made as a result of loitering and community complaints. I told the *Times*, "I agree that they had a very valid point there; and by reducing our numbers to a maximum of three hundred patients at any one site, we are going to avoid that." The most active organization regarding this issue was the Fort Greene Crisis Committee, an umbrella organization of seventy community groups chaired by William L. Graburn, a bank officer, who lived a block away from our Fort Greene clinic. Graburn and his committee remained a thorn in our side for a number of years. He and his group spoke at meetings of local planning boards, wrote letters to newspapers, formally complained to city officials, and in some cases demanded that officials resign. In 1973, the group's complaints were echoed by the Park Slope Addiction Advising and Planning Committee, chaired by Richard Erde, a thirty-three-year-old systems analyst. "The thing is," he remarked at the time, "if the community is unstable and has a large transient population, there is the potential for more crime, and that's what we definitely don't want here." This summed it up. But what to do?

The Fort Greene Committee preferred to see us close and presumably move our patients elsewhere, and clearly other neighborhoods were equally opposed to our presence. Our decision was to decentralize our Fort Greene facility in 1973 by opening a three-story, walk-up clinic in the Bushwick section of Brooklyn, reducing the number of patients who utilized Fort Greene, a change we hoped would mollify the Fort Greene Committee. But no, they *really* wanted us to close.

In time, I realized that part of the hostility from the community may have been my fault. An unnamed official of our organization told the *Times*: "Dr. Primm has done a fine job with his program but an absolutely horrible one with public relations. The Fort Greene clinic poisoned the water because it was far too big, and the doctor became very defensive, if not openly antagonistic. He did not make friends with his attitude." I had wanted ARTC to survive and grow, and in the process, I made a few enemies.

Despite the hostility from community groups, we were able both to meet our expenses and to expand with the strong support we now had from the federal government and from the New York City government. At our founding in 1969, our initial funding of about $1.6 million came from the National Institute of Mental Health, $260,000 from New York City's supplementary budget, and $150,000 from the Model Cities Program in Brooklyn. Our budget for fiscal year September 1, 1972 to August 31, 1973, at the height of the criticism, totaled $2.6 million. Of this amount, about $1.6 million was from the federal government and $932,000 from the city's Addiction Services Agency.

Our federal support was due to the fact that Jerome Jaffe had helped convince the White House that methadone treatment along with drug-free therapy was a promising way to reduce crime, one of Nixon's key policies. We also had the ongoing support of Mayor Lindsay. After visiting a city methadone clinic (at the Beekman Downtown Hospital) in March 1971, he asked New York State to provide $9.2 million to the city's methadone maintenance treatment programs so that, within a year, nine thousand patients could be in treatment. This was extremely ambitious, as the city at the time had fewer than one thousand in methadone treatment. Gordon Chase, the city's Health Services Administrator, said that about three hundred treatment applications were being received weekly, and Lindsay believed that the additional funds were needed "as an essential investment to reduce the hundreds of millions of dollars in crime that now result from heroin addiction." He had made the same calculation as Nixon between drugs and the crime rate, though the two men approached the issue differently. Dudley Morris, deputy commissioner of the city's Addiction Services Agency, the department most responsible for monitoring our activities, was quoted in the *Times* as saying that our organization had proved itself "very valuable." This was a welcome bit of praise.

At this point, our annual funding of $932,000 from the city was not reduced, but approval was delayed. The Board of Estimate, which approved all city expenditures, took more than a month to evaluate the criticism from the community, to wait until our plans for satellite clinics were approved by local planning boards, and to see a favorable audit of our corporation by the city comptroller.

A few months after opening the new clinics, I discussed the transition with the *Amsterdam News*, telling the paper that we had begun with the concept of making all services available at one central location—937 Fulton Street in Fort Greene. As that clinic had grown, services had become uncoordinated and depersonalized, and we finally realized that smaller settings facilitated optimal treatment conditions. And, as mentioned, community complaints about loitering and overcrowding had also played a decisive role.

In 1973, the political landscape changed with the election of Abe Beame as mayor, and the city government's attitude toward drug treatment programs shifted. Beame wanted to show his disagreement with many of John Lindsay's programs, particularly addiction treatment. Shortly after taking the oath of office, Beame appointed Jerome Hornblass commissioner of the city's Addiction Services Agency. Hornblass had previously been an assistant corporation counsel and had worked for Beame in the comptroller's office.

"I had examined the contracts involving drug addiction and drug and alcohol abuse," Hornblass recounted. "We thought the Lindsay administration's rush to create these programs lacked the kind of programmatic and fiscal accountability that was really needed."

This became a tough time for ARTC. Hornblass conducted multiple audits of our finances, putting it out that I had a red phone on my desk to call the president at any time. "It was a nightmare, and everybody knew this because Hornblass was such a political matzo ball," recalled my friend Mitchell Rosenthal, director and founder of Phoenix House, a therapeutic community.

Then came a fresh offensive linking us to Hornblass in an odd way. In August 1974, the Fort Greene Crisis Committee turned its anger against the city government, demanding the resignation of Hornblass. He had, they claimed, "suppressed" an unfavorable audit of ARTC prepared by the comptroller's office, which had "raised the question of possible misuse of large sums of money, possibly running into millions of dollars." The committee called for investigations by the Manhattan and Brooklyn district attorneys. At the time of the audit, Hornblass had been employed in the comptroller's office, doing liaison work with the Addiction Services Agency. A spokesman for Hornblass immediately denied the suppression charge, while a spokesman for the Addiction Services Agency conceded that "some statements made in the audit were certainly questionable, but when examined, they turned out not to be evidence of fraud as far as we can see."

The matter was far from settled. In November 1974, the Fort Greene Crisis Committee demanded further investigation after having obtained a confidential memorandum on the letterhead of the federal Special Action Office for Drug Abuse Prevention to auditors from the Department of Health, Education, and Welfare that alleged "deficiencies and questionable practices" at the Fort Greene clinic. The memo stated that we claimed 60 percent more patients than we had, paid excess laboratory fees, had inadequate office procedures, dispensed methadone without urine samples in 30 percent of the cases, and had a ratio of one employee to every two patients. I told the press that the accusations were "completely erroneous...These charges are constantly being made, in different ways, by different people who want to get us out of the neighborhood."

Defending us against the charges, Robert Dupont, the head of the Special Action Office in Washington, confirmed that the federal grants to ARTC were monitored monthly by his staff, and that he knew of no operating or programmatic irregularities that would cause the grants to be modified.

In 1976, during New York's fiscal crisis, Beame announced that he was going to slash funding significantly for drug treatment programs in the city. A group, calling themselves the City of the Forgotten," camped out in tents in front of Gracie

Mansion. It was good press. Elaine (from Elaine's restaurant) and others came and fed everybody. Beame responded by telling the police commissioner, "Get these people off the sidewalks. This is not good for me." Rosenthal called Howard Rubenstein, New York's PR maven, who called Beame to broker a meeting. Beame's offer was to join Rosenthal at Gracie Mansion without the press, meet the demonstrators, and size things up. As they approached the demonstrators, Beame, a short man, looked up and the group began to sing, on cue: "We love you Abe, oh yes we do." With a tear in his eye, Beame turned to Rosenthal and said, "Dr. Rosenthal, you get much more with sugar than with vinegar."

With that, Beame reversed the city cuts and put his lobbyists in Albany to work with treatment providers in the state capital to discontinue state cuts.

The greatest frustration in the ongoing struggles was that they prevented me from fulfilling my mandate. My goal was to treat 5,000 addicts in New York City: 2,500 in Brooklyn and 2,500 in Harlem. It seemed that there were people who would use any means to block us. When, for example, we found a building at 145th Street and Eighth Avenue and began renovations for a clinic, the building was set on fire. We brought guard dogs to the location, and they killed the dogs. Supposedly a Harlem group called Phase Piggy Back, serious troublemakers, was responsible. They preached a drug-free agenda and wanted no methadone in Harlem. It was the white man's drug, they repeated, enslaving black people. The clinic never opened. (The group is still in operation, although less doctrinaire.) Even people who should have known what was happening on the street were naïve. Danny Cook recalled: "Once Congressman Charlie Rangel and Mayor Abe Beame [mayor from 1974 to 1977] came up to Harlem in an unmarked van and stopped on the corner of 126th street and Eighth Avenue where I grew up. It was ten o'clock at night, and they watched drug sales going on. In the front seat were two cops; Rangel and the mayor were in the back. A guy walks up to the van and asks, 'Do you want to buy some drugs?' And the cop in the front seat asks, 'Do you know who is in the back seat?' And the guy says, 'If he ain't buying drugs, he ain't got no business here.'"

Even in later years, Washington experts on drug abuse seemed unaware of the reality on the street. For example, when Carlton Turner became drug czar under President Reagan and came to New York, Danny was asked to take him around Harlem. They were with a police sergeant and driver, and Danny asked the driver to stop at an illegal numbers hole where a cop was standing. Danny told Turner: "I know that's a numbers hole where they are also selling drugs. The children know it; the cop standing there is the only one who doesn't know it."

In the 1980s, we tried to open a clinic on 116th Street and Lenox Avenue across the street from a mosque. We got planning board and regulatory agency approval and completed renovations. Then the mosque declared that they wouldn't allow us to move in; that they would bodily prevent anyone from entering the building. The mosque refused to back down. In the end, we never opened there.

Earlier, in the 1970s, we moved our administrative offices to 22 Chapel Street, a two-story, brick building on a one-way street in downtown Brooklyn near the Brooklyn Bridge and around the corner from the Cathedral Basilica of Saint James, the see of the Catholic Diocese of Brooklyn. In addition to Fort Greene and Bushwick, we also opened clinics in other areas in Brooklyn and Manhattan: East New York, Upper Third Avenue in Spanish Harlem, 180th Street in Washington Heights, and two clinics on 125th Street in Harlem (which later merged and became the Beny J. Primm Center for a Healthy Lifestyle on 124th Street).

But the opposition, especially in the form of vandalism, often turned the issue of renting space from a molehill into a mountain. Owning buildings provided stability. So because the government funds we received did not allow us to take on mortgages but did allow rent, we created the Affiliated Services and Resources Corporation, a not-for-profit corporation, which held the titles to our facilities and leased the properties to ARTC. In the mid-70s and 80s, property costs were much lower than today, and we were able to purchase buildings, beginning with the Fort Greene facility, which we bought from the Salvation Army in 1974.

The one successful clinic in rented space was at 125th Street, where we expanded when other locations proved unworkable because of opposition. We stayed at 125th Street for about fifteen years until the landlord sold the building and the city tried to move us out. At that point, we had to move to several locations and eventually to 124th Street.

Sadly, staffing problems arose from the nature of our work, at the edges of society. As Tom Rafalsky, ARTC's long-serving attorney, remembers, "Those were the days of the Great Society. Everyone was trying to get a job. You had people who were counselors and heading up aspects of ARTC who were rough-and-ready people. Some were former addicts.

Some weren't credentialed. It was a hard time, getting everyone to work together, to train and create a more professional staff, and to get all the programs at ARTC to operate properly. Today it's different."

At the same time, we had some devoted staff members. My longtime secretary, Maxine Dotson, recalls that "in the mid-1970s, we had severe financial problems when under Mayor Beame funds from the city were delayed. We worked for five days but were paid for only four. But we were so committed to ARTC that if we had to come in on a Saturday, we came in. We didn't earn much money, but the whole concept was different than it is now. We felt a certain way about our clients. We really cared about them. If we were going out for breakfast, we would ask them if they wanted something. We knew all our clients by name."

ARTC was always innovating and looking for new ways to help our diverse, underserved population, which included African American and Hispanic substance abusers; community members from the geographic areas of our clinics; women and men; lesbian, gay, bisexual, and transgender persons; formerly incarcerated individuals; and even those with mental illness. Besides the methadone clinics, we opened other facilities, including some drug-free residential communities. There were two brownstones in the Park Slope area of Brooklyn called Quincy Village that opened in 1971 and were managed by Barbara Gibson, who had been a colleague at Interfaith and then a counselor at ARTC. They were drug-free alternatives to the methadone maintenance clinics and served mainly New York women who had been sent to and released from a public health prison in Fort Worth, Texas, and local men who had been released from the public health prison in Lexington. These people were often homeless. Unfortunately, the surrounding community was up in arms about the program, and after a year and a half, the funding was cut by the Addiction Services Agency of New York City.

Other projects included a poly-drug (the use of two or more psychoactive drugs) program on 132nd Street in Harlem called Coordinated Walk-In, which lasted for about two years. In 1973, we opened a drug-free residential facility in the old Italian Hospital on 110th Street and Central Park West, but after about two years it also closed for financial reasons.

We even started an acupuncture program in 1976 in the belief that it could help addicts. But it too ended for lack of funding.

Whenever possible, we experimented in the area of drug treatment, notably with a LAAM research program in Harlem for about three years starting in 1977. LAMM, or Levo-Alpha Acetyl Methadol, is a medication therapy for individuals addicted to opiates, which provides an alternative to methadone, lasting longer and allowing more time between treatments. Since then, however, LAAM has been taken out of circulation because the manufacturer found it unprofitable.

At one point we decided to try to serve a different clientele and opened a clinic on Sutton Place called Urban Stress Management, which was directed at the white middle class, particularly Wall Street executives addicted to or abusing cocaine, a serious problem in the 70s and 80s that continues today. It was essentially a psychotherapy program. We had a fancy brochure and a beautiful office, but very few clients. It lasted for less than a year. We learned from that experience to stay faithful to our basic mission of helping indigent drug addicts.

In the area of vocational training, ARTC offered GED (General Educational Development) programs, which qualifies the recipient for a high school diploma. It also sponsored one of the first programs for certifying substance abuse counselors. We even created a culinary arts institute to train people for jobs in food preparation. One of the last projects I started at ARTC provided counseling and job training to youths who are incarcerated.

In 2010, ARTC opened an art gallery called Artcurian at our headquarters. The first show, curated by our artists-in-residence Emmett Wigglesworth and Claude Ogundipe Fayomi, was titled "Artists Speaking for the Spirits" and featured forty artists. It was believed to be the largest group of mural-sized paintings ever created by African Diaspora artists. The exhibition was part of a larger project to elicit creativity from people in the women's shelters, particularly children, and at our group homes where people had developmental problems.

By the early 1980s, personal tragedy and professional crises had taken their toll. The pressure from the problems we faced certainly didn't help a condition diagnosed in 1983 as cancer in the upper and middle lobes of my right lung. The lobes were subsequently removed at the Memorial Sloan Kettering Cancer Center. My vital capacity diminished. My breathing diminished. To this day, I easily get out of breath and have to stop and rest.

In 1981, I received a call from the California State Department of Health about a poorly run drug abuse program in Los Angeles called the Hillsman Drug Treatment Center, informally known as Bricks-Kicks, a minority program that was set up as a therapeutic community. They wanted my help. My board of directors agreed to give me a year's sabbatical, and I moved to Los Angeles. From time to time, members of ARTC came out to help me. We established rules and regulations for the Hillsman Center regarding their intakes and follow-up. I also advised the Los Angeles clinics of the Bay Area Addiction Research and Treatment (BAART), a program partially modeled on ARTC. I enjoyed the experience in California, whose treatment climate was mild in comparison to the hothouse atmosphere of New York City.

Chapter Six

New Directions

───── ∞∞∞ ─────

*It is a time not just for compassionate words, but
compassionate action.*

Marian Wright Edelman

By the 1980s, as described above, ARTC had expanded its social services beyond drug abuse treatment. Nonetheless, we found that grantors and donors were reluctant to fund services through us that were unrelated to addiction, even though these programs supported the addict's recovery. To facilitate these programs that we increasingly saw as critical, we decided to create a new entity. In 1981, the Urban Resource Institute (URI), a private, nonprofit corporation, was founded, its purpose to identify and provide direct human services to the underserved populations in the inner city. ARTC and URI shared common management, office space, and trustees, but there were two separate governing boards.

One of the most pressing issues that confronted us was the physical abuse of women and children by addicts. At the time, there were only about four or five women's shelters in New York City, and there was scant information about domestic violence. We decided to fill that void for the families of addicts as well as for families where addiction was not a problem. Louis Bingham, the executive senior vice president of ARTC, together with his wife, Catherine, a deputy commissioner of the Human

Resources Administration of New York City, were instrumental in finding financial resources and staff to start URI's first program, a domestic violence shelter. Of the initial funding finally received by 1984, the state provided about 50 percent, the federal government and the city about 25 percent each. Our first shelter occupied the fifth floor of Harlem Hospital. Again, we had to overcome many misperceptions; and again, the community did not immediately accept us. "'You must be crazy to work with these women' was a typical reaction," said Lorraine Madry, the first director of the program. "We had to educate the community."

In 1987, we purchased two abandoned apartment buildings on East 144th Street from the city for one dollar apiece. We continued the program at Harlem Hospital until 1991, when we received grants from the Federal Housing and Preservation Agency and from New York City's Department of Housing Preservation and Development to renovate the apartment buildings. After finally opening the combined structure in 1992, our program for victims of domestic violence was so successful that Robert Iger, president and chief operating officer of Capital Cities/ABC, gave a grant to the Urban Women's Retreat. Other corporations also provided support, including Bloomberg LP, Bristol-Myers Squibb, and Glaxo Wellcome. Oprah Winfrey contributed $10,000 after visiting the facility.

The Retreat was a vast improvement over the cramped space at Harlem Hospital, where families lived in hospital rooms with communal bathrooms and communal eating facilities. Carmen Smith, then a producer at WABC-TV making a documentary about domestic violence, recalls that she had to use a secret entrance and pass through a basement, a morgue, and puddles of water to get to the shelter at the hospital. (She later became a longtime board member of URI and, as director of corporate outreach for ABC and later as vice president of Creative Imagineering for The Walt Disney Company, was instrumental in arranging grants from both organizations totaling close to $500,000 over the years.)

Located in one of Harlem's roughest neighborhoods, the facility has 44 apartments and 112 beds, providing each family with its own apartment, including a kitchen and a bathroom. "There was a crack house across the street," said Lorraine Madry. "From the top floors of our building you could watch the drug deals. The building was close to the border between the Jamaican drug gangs and the Harlem drug gangs. I was leery of coming to work. But despite my fears for my staff and myself, nothing ever happened, and the community slowly supported us. People were not supposed to know where our shelter was, but they knew. When one of our women was challenged by her abuser on the corner and was slapped around by him, people in the neighborhood saw this and beat that man so badly he never came back."

There are literally thousands of stories from women we have helped. Rosa (not her real name) left Puerto Rico in 1981 with one of her three daughters to find work in New York. After several years, she moved in with a man who soon started to abuse her, choking and hitting her while she was pregnant. As the months passed, he not only beat her but also kept her locked in the apartment and took the telephone with him so that she couldn't call anyone. One day in the early 90s, her daughter discovered where the man had hidden the key to their apartment, and Rosa quickly fled with her children. A neighbor had given her the telephone number of our twenty-four-hour hotline, where she was directed to one of our shelters in Manhattan. "They told me what to do," she said. "The shelter made it as easy as possible for my children. My daughter was thrilled when they gave her a doll she wanted."

Our staff arranged a police escort to accompany Rosa to her apartment to retrieve her belongings, helped her obtain a court order of protection, and arranged income from public assistance. Rosa participated in individual and group therapy sessions at the shelter, later saying, "I learned things in the groups that I never knew. I never thought about all the other kinds of abuse, not only physical and mental but financial and sexual." Before she left the shelter in 1995, she was hired by URI as a housing specialist. Her job is to counsel women about housing and help with applications. "I arrived with nothing," she said. "URI gave me the tools to turn my life around."

In 2001 we opened a second shelter in Brooklyn called Safe Haven with 32 apartments for 120 residents. URI now has four emergency domestic violence shelters, including a second in Manhattan and one in

Brooklyn, where women can stay from 90 to 135 days, as well as a transitional shelter for women who have exhausted their stay but need more time. Our shelter program remains on the forefront of domestic violence intervention through a research and evaluation unit that conducts studies relating to domestic violence; it also hosts an annual domestic violence conference. The URI shelters have eventually come to serve over a thousand women and children annually. In the 1990s, our hotline was turning down about a thousand women a month.

Another program that grew out of our social services outreach was the Urban Center for the Developmentally Disabled. Located in the East New York section of Brooklyn, this was a job-training program for young adults with developmental disabilities after they have aged out of the public school system. Since its inception in 1985, over one hundred people have been placed in such jobs as stock clerk, airport customer escort, cargo area worker, and nurse's aide.

Later, when the Willowbrook State School closed down in 1987 following an exposé in the press of its mistreatment of hundreds of mentally disabled residents, the New York State Office of Mental Retardation found that it needed transportation services for people with disabilities. As we had already served young adults with developmental disabilities, it seemed logical for us to offer transportation as well. Hazel Dukes, the president of the New York State chapter of NAACP, helped us with the proposal, and we put in a bid to transport people in all boroughs (except Staten Island) from their homes to their day programs. We were awarded the project with a one million dollar grant from the state and contracted with bus companies to provide the services that we would monitor.

As our reputation grew, the state approached us as a minority organization to take on the project of group homes. Awarded a contract, we opened our first group home for the developmentally disabled in 2000. Currently, URI manages three such homes in Queens: the Linden Residence, the Beny J. Primm residence, and the Ferndale Residence.

Our expansion developed not from a master plan but from the ad hoc needs of our client population. As a not-for-profit organization, we had to rely on the largesse of federal, state, and city governments and of private donors. Expanding ARTC and URI was never easy or simple. I needed the financial and political resources of the white establishment as well as the political connections of the black establishment. Through my work in New York and Washington, I made professional connections to Republican political leaders, which helped with government funding. But membership in black social groups also played a crucial role in my ability to represent and advance the interests of people written off by the power structure. Prominent black organizations were composed of lawyers, doctors, and politicians who came to understand the value and promote the legitimacy of our drug abuse work and later of our HIV/AIDS programs.

In the early 1970s, I was regularly invited to gatherings hosted by Dr. M. Moran Weston, pastor of Saint Philip's Church in Harlem and one of the founders of the Carver Federal Savings Bank. About fifteen people attended the monthly breakfast meetings, which brought together some of New York's leading black professionals, including Congressman Charles Rangel; Percy Sutton, who became borough president; and David Dinkins, who became mayor. These friendships and others helped me navigate the perilous waters of New York City politics. Also of help was membership in social and service clubs, including the 100 Black Men of America, a social organization whose membership is mainly based on professional accomplishments; Sigma Pi Phi, known as "the Boulé," a social fraternity; and the Guardsmen, a social organization composed mainly of physicians and attorneys. I have also been an active member for thirty-five years of the Fellas, a social organization that awards scholarships.

Lawrence Otis Graham, author of *Our Kind of People: Inside America's Black Upper Class*, described these as "exclusive hard-to-crack social groups." As lineage is difficult to determine precisely for most African Americans, membership is mostly associated with certain colleges and universities: Fisk, Howard, Morehouse, Hampton, Morgan State, and Lincoln. I had attended Lincoln University and graduated from West Virginia State College. My social world consisted of people I had met at these schools and through the Alpha Phi Alpha fraternity, as well as through Saint Mark's Church, Dewitt Clinton High School, the army, and, perhaps most important, Martha's Vineyard, where I've spent the month of August every year since 1972.

I first visited the Vineyard in the 1960s as a guest of Preston Powell, a close friend from high school and the son of the late Harlem Congressman Adam Clayton Powell Jr. and Isabel Powell. Oak Bluffs on the Vineyard has become, over time, the preferred summer destination for established African Americans, in no small part because the Powells invited their wide circle of friends to visit starting in the 1940s. "African Americans have been an integral part of life and culture on Martha's Vineyard for more than three centuries," writes my friend and historian Robert Hayden in his *African Americans on Martha's Vineyard*. "Unlike Martha's Vineyard, other historic black resort areas like Highland Beach and Idlewild were formed and developed by a deliberate and planned black initiative—that is, in direct response to race discrimination in America...The black presence on Martha's Vineyard developed alongside, parallel to and in conjunction with, the white community." Oak Bluffs still encompasses one of the country's oldest circles of black wealth and power.

These connections and lifelong friendships from my school years onward were not only personally and socially fulfilling but also helped in countless ways to advance my work. But at the same time, I realized early on that to be effective in the inner cities, I had to understand the lives of street people and be on positive terms even with some on the fringes of the law. There was Raymond "Bumpy" Johnson, for example, whose racketeering career was featured in several films, including Shaft and The Cotton Club. Bumpy met me through a niece. He trusted me and knew that I wasn't a threat to him or his business. In his way, he protected our neighborhood drug treatment programs and me. I would occasionally see Bumpy at a bar at Lenox Terrace where he lived as well as at his hangout, Wells Restaurant on 132nd Street and Seventh Avenue, where he collapsed and died one Sunday morning in July 1968.

When I occasionally stopped at certain bars in Harlem, I would notice drug dealers. They knew of my work for our people and kept hands off. It may be hard to grasp, but local drug pushers on the street sometimes paid for substance abuse treatment—for kids, for example, whom they knew had become strung out. Nor was this phenomenon unique to New York City. Oddly enough, it is often the guy selling the most who is helping a specific facility, individual, or youth group.

I can say after many years that I know addicts and don't fear them, though in the early days, just to be safe, I hired a tough guy from the streets named Nolan Johnson, who let it be known that no one should mess with me. I've learned their culture and language and the behavioral patterns of inner city addicts that are consistent everywhere—their style of communication, their social network, their posture, their response when they get high, the way they nod. In the field and the community, this is called "addictiveness." I coined the phrase "addictdom," the kingdom of addicts, to describe the world of addictive behavior with its own unwritten laws. Amazingly, addicts abide by these laws: you don't welch or squeal, for example.

I treat them with respect, and they return that respect. They might rip somebody off the minute I turn my back, but not me. No addict has ever threatened me with a knife, a gun, or with any violence. In fact, they've been so appreciative of my work that I would find TVs and other gifts in my parked car, which I would return with a respectful explanation.

The notable exception to the consistent behavioral traits of the addict, however, was Vietnam. Those who became addictive there usually did not learn the nodding and the accompanying syndrome of addicts here. The "shooting galleries" for addiction in Vietnam were quite different from those in our inner cities. Soldiers on the war front hid their behavior even when addicted to drugs far more potent than those available in the United States. In Vietnam, if a soldier nodded or displayed behavior associated with addiction, he would be immediately revealed; he knew that, if caught, he would be in dire trouble.

Finally, from a racial perspective, it's fascinating to me that on the street white and blacks addicts share everything; the drug experience is a kind of leveling where there is complete integration among fellow travelers. But once in treatment and improving, they go their separate ways, back to their communities and racially separate lives.

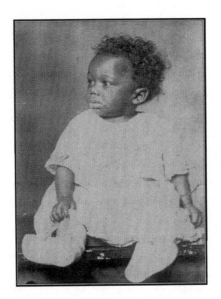

Me, one-and-a-half-years-old.

My late wife Annie Delphine Evans Primm.

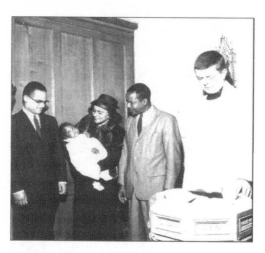

The christening of Annelle in Switzerland with godfather Ralph Waldo Fenderson, godmother Eldorado Johnson to my right, and the Rev. Gerald B. O'Grady of the American church in Geneva to my left.

I was manager of the Dewitt Clinton basketball team in 1944; Dolph Schayes, who later became a star NBA player and coach, is seated, second from right.

From my high school yearbook:
"Shorty, To become an MD, Sine Labor Nihil."

BENNY J. PRIMM

Nickname: "Bee Jay"
1622 Sedgwick Ave.
New York City
Degree Sought: B.S. in Educa-
  tion
Activities: Alpha Phi Alpha
  Fraternity
Future Plans: To be an M. D.

My college yearbook entry.

The army transformed me from a boy into a man.

Being congratulated for leading the best platoon in the artillery division of the 82nd Airborne.

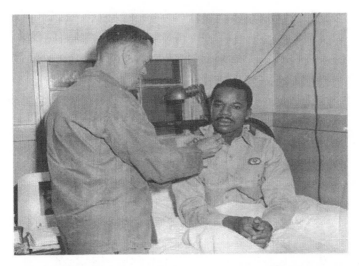

Being promoted to first lieutenant after my automobile accident.

Mayor John Lindsay was instrumental in providing funds to start the Addiction Research and Treatment Corporation (ARTC); Dr. Bertram S. Brown, director of the National Institute of Mental Health, is standing.

In the early years of ARTC, flyers circulated in neighborhood barber shops with this picture of me and the caption: "Heroin isn't the only drug and the pusher comes in many disguises."

Conferring with President Nixon at San Clemente in 1971 after returning from Vietnam; counterclockwise: Egil "Bud" Krogh, Dr. Jerome Jaffe, President Nixon, John Erlichman, myself.

Meeting with President Reagan and Nancy Reagan during her "Just Say No" campaign.

President George H. W. Bush appointed me associate administrator of the Office of Treatment Improvement, which oversaw all drug abuse treatment in the nation.

Declaring a state of escalating crisis, President Bill Clinton in 1998 pledged funding for minority AIDS programs.

To Dr. Beny Primm
With best wishes,

President George W. Bush appointed me to the President's Advisory Council on HIV and AIDS in 2003.

A profile in the Daily News, February 21, 2005.

Coretta Scott King was a strong supporter of our work combating HIV/ AIDS in the minority community.

Discussing with Jackie Robinson in approximately 1970 how members of unions could receive treatment for drug abuse.

With Mayor David Dinkins and Magic Johnson at an ARTC award ceremony in approximately 2000.

My longtime administrative aide and frequent companion Barbara Gibson.

With Barbara Gibson and Romare Bearden who is signing a lithograph of his original collage "Here Begins Medicine" in my honor. I gave copies to the Morehouse School of Medicine, Meharry Medical College, Howard University Medical School, Charles R. Drew University of Medicine and Science, and the Sophie Davis School of Biomedical Education.

To my left, my daughters Annelle (the eldest), Martine, and Jeanine.

With Dr. David Satcher and my granddaughter India on the occasion of my receiving the surgeon general's medal.

My daughter Eraka Bath Fortuit and my granddaughter Noa Fortuit.

With my finacee Ellena Stone Huckaby.

Chapter Seven

A Return to Washington

At the banquet table of nature, there are no reserved seats. You get what you can take, and you keep what you can hold. If you can't take anything, you won't get anything, and if you can't hold anything, you won't keep anything. And you can't take anything without organization.

A. Philip Randolph

From the moment I joined Jerry Jaffe on his trip to Vietnam in 1971 to investigate addiction in the army, I had one foot in the world of drug abuse in New York's inner-city areas and the other in the rarefied world of Washington, DC. I shuttled between the streets of the addicted poor and the halls of power where I advocated for them.

Although I had not supported Jimmy Carter in the campaign for his election in 1976, I remained an informal consultant to the Special Action Office after Peter Bourne became drug czar, offering advice and input whenever it was requested and serving on advisory committees. Bourne thought that my willingness to work with both the Nixon and Carter administrations made me "the most important spokesperson for the black community in terms of drug abuse treatment and in circles where there was still controversy about methadone maintenance." With the election of Ronald Reagan in 1980, however, drug abuse treatment was sidelined. As soon as the votes were counted, an organization called the National Federation of Parents for Drug-Free Youth led a massive letter-writing campaign to President-elect Reagan, asking him to appoint Carlton Turner to the White House as his drug-policy advisor. Turner, of the University of Mississippi, was responsible for growing much of the marijuana used in scientific research throughout the world. Having educated parents at various conferences about the pharmacological effects of marijuana on the brain and body, he had earned their trust. Acting on the parent federation's appeals, Reagan quickly selected Turner as his drug czar.

Shortly after the inauguration, Turner helped the federation arrange for parent-group leaders to brief Nancy Reagan on the prevention movement and enlist her support for their cause. She not only responded positively but also served informally as the national spokesperson for the parent drug-prevention movement, emphasizing the "Just Say No" slogan to discourage children from engaging in illegal use. The phrase was absorbed into the culture and was frequently mocked, although illegal recreational drug use did decline during the Reagan years.

We had swung from Nixon's crime-prevention and Vietnam-based motivations for federally supported drug abuse treatment programs to Reagan's decision that, under the New Federalism, the federal government should limit its role in domestic health issues. Reagan told the states that provision of services was now their responsibility. The federal government would fund drug abuse research only, terminate many treatment programs, and give the states block grants, enabling them to decide for themselves how to allocate the money. In addition to shifting resources to the states, the administration also shifted federal directives concerning drug abuse from the White House to the Justice Department, where Attorney General Edwin Meese became hell-bent on rounding up, prosecuting, and imprisoning drug dealers—the more the better.

In 1986, Len Bias, an all-American college basketball player at the University of Maryland, selected by the Boston Celtics as the second overall pick in the NBA draft, died of cardiac arrhythmia caused by a cocaine overdose. His death drew a lot of media attention and heightened public awareness. The national epidemics of crack cocaine and HIV increasingly demanded attention, and pressure grew from Democrats in Congress, particularly from Senator Edward Kennedy and California Congressman Henry Waxman, to fund services.

When Polly Gault, the executive director of the Presidential Commission on the Human Immunodeficiency Virus Epidemic, established by President Reagan in 1987, joined George Bush's campaign team in the lead-up to the primaries, she immediately recommended me as advisor. The vice president requested a meeting with me, asking that I bring in a team experienced in substance abuse to discuss an agenda he could adopt should he win the nomination. This was a clear sign that he intended, if elected, to restore the federal role in both public policy around substance abuse and in direct involvement in funding and organizing the provision of services. As I saw it, this was extremely good news. Our group met with him in Washington for two and a half hours.

In 1988, George Bush invited me to join him in a little town on the Mississippi river and ride down on a riverboat to the Republican National Convention in New Orleans. There were about ten black folk on board. I spent most of the time talking to the president's brothers. Since then, friends and colleagues have ribbed me about my riverboat excursion. They don't all know that during the convention, I also had a brief discussion about Vietnam at a cocktail party with Senator Strom Thurmond, the infamous segregationist.

Following President Bush's election, I was named to the National Drug Abuse Advisory Council and asked to become associate administrator of the Office of Treatment Improvement (OTI), later called the Center for Substance Abuse Treatment, which oversaw all drug treatment in the nation. (The Special Action Office for Drug Abuse Prevention—later the Drug Abuse Policy Office, then the Office of National Drug Control Policy—was the policy arm of the White House where the drug czars held sway; funds were distributed through the Alcohol Drug Abuse and Mental Health Administration (ADAMHA) and its Office of Treatment Improvement. To work in the latter, I had to give up my advisory functions in the former.)

At first I was reluctant and expressed my hesitation to Dr. Fred Goodwin, head of ADAMHA and my prospective boss. "This is what we want," he told me. "We will borrow you from ARTC and pay your current salary while you are in Washington under what is known as special expert authority. You will maintain ties to your organization and be hired on an expedited basis. And we will cover your travel and moving expenses." The leaders of ARTC simply said, "Do it." And so in 1990, I was appointed by the Secretary of Health and Human Services to direct the Federal Government's Office of Treatment Improvement. My responsibilities included the development of programs and support relating to the treatment of addictive disorders in the United States and its territories.

Under Reagan, as I've described, the federal government focused on research and enforcement and transferred delivery of treatment services to the states. Bush reversed the process, returning treatment services to the federal arena. Unfortunately, a rift appeared between research and development around resources. There was resentment at the National Institute of Drug Abuse (NIDA) when some funds were withdrawn to fund my office. But I retained influence at NIDA and in the substance abuse community nationwide through my memberships in the American College of Neuropsychopharmacology and the College on Problems of Drug Dependence, an independent scientific society. This influence enabled me to bring together researchers and treatment providers, a critical part of my role. It also helped that I brought some color into our office at Rockwall II, a glass and aluminum tower in Rockville, Maryland.

By the end of 1989, we had our office space, but our operation had to be built from scratch. With an initial staff of fourteen people, we grew to twenty-seven within nine months, including my longtime friend and colleague Jerry Jaffe. By the time I left on February 25, 1993, we had expanded to 160 people, with an annual budget of about one billion dollars.

The minute I assumed responsibility in my new capacity under President Bush, I was faced with the mess created by the block grant system that had been in existence under the Reagan presidency. At that point, almost 90 percent of our budget was for block grants, the remainder for discretionary funding. The block grants provided a rich breeding ground for misuse of funds and overall lack of accountability. As we looked into the matter, we found that states were using the funds however they saw fit. There were no standards.

My top administrative aides were Dr. Warren Hewitt and Lisa Scheckel Levy. She remembers, "We had to get some teeth in our ability to regulate the states. They had been given a blank check for so long, you can imagine how resistant they were. And the federal government had never followed up on how the states had used the block grant money. They were required to submit a report each year with no format, no baseline, and no specific content. It was all over the map. There was no ability to compare growth or achievement in any domain. We didn't even know how many treatment programs there were in the country."

We discovered that Maryland was using block grant money to buy uniforms for state-employee softball teams and to entertain the Olympic committee on the Eastern Shore. One person was prosecuted and given a prison term. Among other things, he had provided his niece a college scholarship from government funds and purchased cars from an uncle's dealership.

But, as often in my past work, I again encountered resistance. I think the bureaucrats must have thought, "Here's this guy coming in, telling us what to do." I was outspoken and I was black, and politics and turf considerations were always in play. First, the administration saddled me with Robert Trachtenberg, a career bureaucrat and Fred Goodwin's deputy, to monitor my influence on policy. My immediate superior, he had been under heat from Congress for inaction. So, while he complied with the creation of the Office of Treatment Improvement and hired me, he intended to build a Potemkin village. It hadn't occurred to Fred Goodwin that I would work to change the entire treatment delivery system and that I had the support of President Bush and Louis Sullivan, the Secretary of Health and Human Services. Lisa Scheckel Levy recalled that "everybody assumed that at any given moment" I could just pick up the phone and call my friend Louis Sullivan if I was having problems. I never did. That wasn't my style, to go up the line. But the perception worked in our favor.

White House support and perceptions of access notwithstanding, obstacles remained. First, Trachtenberg took a dislike to me. I had written a memo mentioning duplicity, a term frowned upon in government. Trachtenberg shot back a barbed memo: "How dare you write anything like this. If this was a different kind of place, I would take you to the gym."

I couldn't help but remember the thugs from Nat's Coming who had threatened me in my ARTC office and responded to Trachtenberg, "If ever you want to take me to the gym, you'd better bring your lunch." Mostly, Trachtenberg employed trivial complaints. Barbara Gibson, my chief assistant at ARTC, had signed my name to a document. Trachtenberg and his fiscal officer, Joe Leon, claimed a conflict of interest and notified the Inspector General and the FBI. Barbara explained to the FBI that she had signed the document on my behalf concerning a routine matter related to a grant decided upon before I had gone to work for the government. When the agents interviewed Barbara at ARTC and seemed inclined to persist, she asked, "What are you going to do? Handcuff me and take me to jail?"

The investigation ended there with no action taken.

Among my greatest accomplishments in Washington was establishing comprehensive drug abuse treatment throughout the United States and the territories. I effectively pressed the case that, because many addicts suffer from high blood pressure, diabetes, and many other conditions, comprehensive care, including full health care, was the best way to deliver drug treatment. I also stressed integrating HIV identification and care into substance abuse programs. This I believed was critical. My policy of comprehensiveness influenced the whole country but didn't catch on as much as I would have liked because of the expense of its implementation. Another area of great pride was a conference I sponsored called the Linkage Initiative where all the agencies of government concerned with substance abuse came together. It was managed by Dr. Saul Levin, recently named medical director of the American Psychiatric Association.

In addition, I increased representation from Native Americans, Hispanics, and blacks in the grant process and as recipients of federal aid. Among our other lasting legacies were an emphasis on HIV treatment; stricter oversight for methadone treatment under Robert Lubran, an assistant I had hired in 1989; and an attempt to address healthcare disparities in underserved populations. One of our most important achievements, highly relevant today, was to translate research into practice through the Treatment Improvement Protocols (TIPS), known as "best practice guidelines," in the areas of alcohol and drug abuse. We assembled experts from around the country, and they spent days drafting protocols, including guidelines for state methadone programs; specialized treatment for pregnant and substance-abusing women and for alcohol- and drug-abusing adolescents; screening for infectious diseases among substance abusers; and broadened treatment of patients with coexisting mental illness. There are currently over fifty Treatment Improvement Protocols, including "Managing Chronic Pain in Adults With or In Recovery From Substance Abuse Disorders" and "Behavioral Health Services for People Who Are Homeless." These protocols are available to anyone on the web and are used by treatment centers around the world.

Our work was successful in part because the timing was right. Substance abuse was a bright neon sign in the public psyche where it was associated with crime, prisoners, and, of course, HIV/AIDS. Political and economic pressures also mattered, to the extent that in 1991 our division, which was addressing public concerns about substance abuse and its fallout, received an increase in its discretionary grant budget from the National Institutes of Health, while other branches of NIH received no increase at all.

With Clinton's election, I resigned, and my deputy, Lisa Scheckel Levy, took over. In our total six-year span, our office excelled. I am extremely proud to have put my imprimatur on comprehensive treatment throughout the nation and grateful that treatment centers could offer people what they needed to repair their broken lives.

Sue Becker, director of policy planning and legislation and then of state programs at my agency, recalled that I "created a framework that has lasted for twenty years," though it "wasn't easy" to be on my staff. I would typically return from one of my trips, say from the south side of Detroit, and would call everyone into my office to announce: "The south side of Detroit needs such and such, and I want to see a plan in two days." Apparently, I "wanted to fix the whole world."

Chapter Eight

Plague

———— ∞∞∞ ————

This man was out here before anybody.

Earvin "Magic" Johnson

In 1983, I encountered a fatal disease among my patients. While examining a man at the Harlem clinic, I discovered swellings under his arms and in his groin. I advised a biopsy; he refused, soon developed pneumonia, and died. I learned later that he was infected with HIV. It was the first case I had encountered, but it would not be the last, as increasing numbers of my patients were contracting this mysterious and deadly illness that soon became known as HIV/AIDS.

Acquired immune deficiency syndrome (AIDS) is a disease of the immune system caused by the human immunodeficiency virus (HIV). AIDS is the advanced form of HIV infection. At the time, it was believed that the disease mainly affected the four Hs— homosexuals, hemophiliacs, heroin addicts, and Haitians. It spread among homosexuals through sexual contact; among hemophiliacs through blood transfusion; and early on, the assumption was that drug abusers had contracted the disease through prostitution, sexual activity, and drug injection. This was the understanding we had of our patients.

The explanation as to why Haitians had a higher incidence of infection than people from other countries was a bit more complex. In the

1960s, many Haitians sought employment in the newly independent Congo because the main language was French, as in Haiti. Most of these migrants were male, and it's assumed that they contracted the virus from interaction with Congolese prostitutes, bringing the virus back with them. Then, in the decades that followed, Haiti became a prime destination for gay tourists. (One theory, since overturned by the National Academy of Sciences, blamed a promiscuous Canadian flight attendant named Gaetan Dugas for spreading the virus in the west.)

I became passionate about combating the terrible plague affecting my patients. Historically, African Americans have suffered from much poorer health than Caucasians. This is due to a variety of historical and social circumstances, including the legacy of slavery, the abuse of medical experimentation, and the unequal access to health care, which led to much higher death rates from cancer and chronic illnesses. In the 1980s, these disparities converged in the HIV/AIDS epidemic.

By 1984 and 1985, as tests became more widely available, I found that over 40 percent of patients at ARTC were positive. Since the growing prevalence of the disease in the drug abuse community was not being addressed, we reached out beyond the addicts in our programs to educate the wider community. In 1984, I convened a meeting of about twenty-five leaders of drug abuse programs, infectious disease doctors, and city government officials at our Brooklyn headquarters on Chapel Street to discuss action against the growing menace of HIV/AIDS among the populations we served. A colleague, Elaine Greeley, recalls, "At the time, people were dying in the streets, even on the ledges in front of Kings County Medical Center. Some officials wanted to quarantine people with HIV on barges in the river, and many didn't believe it was a real problem. We went to see a number of city council members and a couple of times were thrown out of their offices. They thought it had nothing to do with the black or Latino communities, that it was a gay disease. So no one was doing anything to help."

As early as 1986, I knew and stated that the disease would be transmitted through the intravenous drug abuse community in shooting galleries and that it would adversely affect minorities. I called people to arms. In

1986, I created the Brooklyn AIDS Task Force with a $300,000 grant from the AIDS Institute of the New York State Department of Health. For its first four years, it was based at our ARTC headquarters, where I became the first chairman of the board. Elaine Greeley, who had run a residential treatment program, became executive director.

From the original staff of five, the task force, now known as Bridging Access to Care, has grown to eighty and has served more than 100,000 people, with a broad mandate of educating high-risk populations of adolescents, women substance abusers, and incarcerated people; providing mobile community HIV testing and syringe distribution; and offering mental health services, substance abuse treatment services, and primary medical care. The Brooklyn AIDS Task Force has become a model for similar groups across the country.

The following year, in 1987, I helped found and then became chair of the board of the National Minority Aids Council, the main national organization focusing on the epidemic in communities of color. The impetus for the group occurred when Craig Harris, a gay African American with AIDS, rushed onto the stage shouting "I will be heard" during a panel at the American Public Health Association's first AIDS workshop in 1986, to which no one of color had been invited to participate. Our organization's first order of business was an informational meeting with US Surgeon General C. Everett Koop, which had been scheduled to last fifteen minutes. Koop, unaware of the ravage of HIV/AIDS among minorities, sat riveted for nearly two and a half hours. Today, the National Minority AIDS Council fulfills its mission through education, conferences, treatment, and research programs.

Then, in 1988, I became a vice chair of the National Black Leadership Commission on AIDS (NBLCA), which had been founded by Debra Fraser-Howze a year before to conduct research and advocacy on HIV/AIDS and other health disparities. With affiliates in cities throughout the United States where African American communities were hardest hit by the HIV/AIDS epidemic, the organization was well positioned to make a difference.

As my research and advocacy continued, I feverishly warned about the dangers of HIV infection, the importance of safe sex, and the urgency of testing. I spoke at universities and on the radio and traveled across the country with Magic Johnson on and off for a year, speaking at schools and churches in such places as Birmingham, Miami, and Chicago. The travel was sponsored in part by GlaxoSmithKline and by Abbot Laboratories. It was a horrible time for individuals thought to be responsible for this dreadful disease that had no cure.

During this period, I also spoke at international conferences on substance abuse and was a representative to the World Health Organization and a delegate to UNESCO conferences. I advised governments in Holland, Kenya, South Africa, and Nigeria, where I visited prisons and drug treatment programs. I often traveled to the Virgin Islands under the auspices of the Department of Health and Human Services to set up drug treatment programs. As a member of the International Conference for Ministers of Health on AIDS Prevention, I traveled with Secretary of Health and Human Services Dr. Louis Sullivan to London, where we met the Queen and Prime Minister Margaret Thatcher.

By 1987, AIDS was high on the national agenda. President Ronald Reagan created the Presidential Commission on the Human Immunodeficiency Virus Epidemic, chaired by Admiral James Watkins. I was appointed to the commission on the recommendation of Dr. Burton Lee III, Vice President George H. W. Bush's physician, who had seen an interview with me on the topic of addiction. I was also helpful to the commission by calming ACT-UP and other groups who disrupted its meetings. In Miami, for example, a Haitian group burst into our meeting and tried to take it over. I assured them in French that I would secure "the kind of attention you deserve from this commission." The Haitians not only backed off but even invited me to their homes.

I contributed to the commission's report with recommendations regarding addicts who were also infected with HIV: "Because a clear federal, state, and local government policy is needed, the Commission recommends a national policy of providing 'treatment on demand' for intravenous drug users." This controversial conclusion stressed treatment rather than law enforcement.

In the late 1980s, I asked Dr. Lawrence Brown, then the senior executive vice president of ARTC, to expand our programs of HIV services and HIV testing. The trauma and fear of being tested for the disease cannot be overstated. In this regard, a grant from the AIDS Institute of the New York State Department of Health enabled us to fund a project to include partner notification, HIV individual and group counseling, testing, and AIDS education, principally for people of the street, often homeless and unemployed, certainly without access to medical information.

In line with my certainty that the two were related, we were among the first, along with Don Des Jarlais at Beth Israel, to do research on the connection between drug abuse and HIV/AIDS. The only community-based drug treatment program studying the illness in the mid-80s, ARTC collaborated with academic and other research institutions, such as the National Academy of Sciences and the National Institutes of Health. We were thought to be the largest non-university-based facility conducting such research, particularly as it affected the black community. Our focus was on the behavior associated with substance abuse, HIV, and its transmission. Researchers' ideas at the time about behaviors linking HIV and drug use were so vague as to be useless in the development of prevention programs. Was the heightened incidence of HIV a result of drug use itself? Was it the manner in which the drug was used, or the context of drug use and the sharing of needles and other drug paraphernalia? We compiled detailed questionnaires and compared infected patients with those who were not infected. Dr. Brown and I published our research findings in a number of medical journals, including *The New England Journal of Medicine, The Journal of Substance Abuse,* and in monographs published by the National Institute on Drug Abuse. Our findings and those of other investigators led to mounting evidence that the disease among addicts was transmitted more often by drug use than by sexual acts.

As the incidence of HIV grew among the community of intravenous drug users in New York City during the mid-1980s, I zeroed in on the sharing of drug injection equipment, or the "works," a practice motivated by convenience, friendship, and ritual. Despite some concern about the spread of hepatitis, there was little reluctance to share equipment prior to the appearance of AIDS in the late 70s and early 80s. According to a seminal 1988 study by the National Institute of Drug Abuse, "The first cases of AIDS in New York have been retrospectively diagnosed as occurring in 1978, with the first cases in IV drug users appearing in 1980...Men who engaged in homosexual activity as well as injecting drugs appear to have been the bridge group to spread the virus from homosexuals who did not inject drugs to heterosexual IV drug users."

Transmission of HIV among intravenous drug users who share their equipment comes from contaminated blood left on needles, cookers, syringes, cotton, or other paraphernalia. The rapid spread of HIV among sharing, intravenous drug users in New York was the result of three related factors. A relatively large number of homosexual men injected drugs and shared equipment with heterosexual drug users; an increasing availability of heroin and cocaine in the late 1970s led to a general increase in drug injection; and the prevalence of shooting galleries, the sharing of "house works," and the selling of blood for transfusion readily spread the virus.

At a shooting gallery, typically located in or near "copping areas" (where drugs can be easily purchased), the user rents drug injection equipment from the proprietor of the space for a small fee (typically one or two dollars in New York City in the early 80s). After use, the equipment is returned for rental to the next customer. The needle and syringe are used repeatedly until the needle becomes too dull for further use or the syringe becomes clogged. Similarly, house works are lent to customers by small-scale dealers when the drugs are purchased and returned to the dealer after use to then be passed to the next buyer.

Because sharing of works was so implicated in disease transmission by intravenous drug users, the discussion for decades centered on the policy of needle exchange, whereby unused needles are given to drug abusers by outside organizations. Controls regarding needle exchanges required that used needles be turned in for new ones. But I feared that the lack of sufficient control and oversight would simply flood the streets with used needles. And so I remained publicly opposed to needle exchange. I changed my mind after a visit to Holland in 1988 at the invitation of the

Dutch Ministry of Health, where I watched as they distributed needles and syringes. With that, and the realization that HIV was spinning out of control in the black community, jumping from addicts to their families, I made a 180-degree turn and accepted needle and syringe exchanges—if done with proper supervision.

Of course, like others, I have wondered if I worked enough against this plague. In 2002, former President Clinton reflected in theNew York Times: "Do I wish I could have done more? Yes, but I do not know that I could have done it." In particular, he cited his administration's refusal in 1998, after a bitter internal debate, to lift a longstanding ban on federal financing for programs to distribute clean needles to drug addicts, even as top government scientists said such programs did not encourage drug abuse and could save lives. "I think I was wrong about that," he concluded. "I should have tried harder to do that." Clinton's advisers had feared political disaster from a lift of the ban, and they thought Republicans would pass legislation stripping federal money from groups providing free needles.

A turning point in our fight against AIDS, and a perfect example of the kind of personal involvement required to produce effective policies and secure funding, occurred in the late 1990s, a pivotal moment in the history of federal support for minority victims of the disease. In early March 1998, a group of AIDS researchers and activists had been invited to the Centers for Disease Control (CDC) in Atlanta, Georgia, to meet with Dr. Helene Gayle, director of the CDC's National Center for HIV, STD, and TB Prevention, and Claire Broome, the acting CDC director. The federal government and the CDC in particular had remained on the sidelines as the epidemic increased among African Americans, while minority activism had also remained, surprisingly, somewhat dormant.

"It took so long from '87 to '98 because everyone was dying," recalled Paul Kawata, a founder and executive director of the National Minority AIDS Council. "Our whole lives were spent at hospitals and funerals. We had no realistic drug treatment. Then about '96 or '97 we got protease inhibitors. They changed the course of the epidemic and gave us a moment to breathe, a moment to ask, 'How do we change things?'"

A kind of elder statesman of the AIDS advocacy movement, I had been asked by my colleagues in Atlanta to be their spokesperson at the CDC meeting. I said that I would be happy to stand in the background and help in any way I could, but that it was time for younger people to take leadership positions. "Do this one last hurrah," they urged.

As the CDC meeting opened on March 8, I settled into a conference room at the Wyndham Garden Hotel in suburban Atlanta, along with thirty-three black AIDS doctors, advocates, and ministers. After three decades of advising on federal drug policy, I understood that most government agencies had been conditioned to perform a subtle two-step to minimize any information that might anger the black community. But this time I felt that the CDC had been boxed into an inordinately cautious approach in its handling of AIDS in black America. It struck me as a backward racial and health policy, although I'd had enough contact with the CDC over the years to know that there wasn't any racist agenda at work.

Under these circumstances, it would have been reasonable for the attendees, as they prepared to listen to the CDC staffers run through the epidemiological numbers, to expect little from the conference. But this meeting was different. A few weeks earlier, Dr. Gayle had instructed her staff to imbue this conference with a sense of urgency. This certainly had its effect on me. I had been studying the AIDS epidemic for more than ten years. That afternoon the graph data included one startling new statistic: every hour, seven Americans were infected with HIV and three of them were black. "African Americans make up 3 percent of the United States population," theNew York Times wrote afterward. "But they account for about 57 percent of all new infections with human immunodeficiency virus, which causes AIDS, according to the Centers for Disease Control and Prevention. Among people aged thirteen to twenty-four, the estimate, based on data collected from twenty-five states between January 1994 and June 1997, is even higher: 63 percent."

The first day was marked by the anger and frustration of our group. I thought of ACT-UP, the AIDS Coalition to Unleash Power, who had attended and disrupted the presidential commission's meetings and often been removed by security, and who marched on the Capitol steps and lay down in front of buses. The only person of color on the commission, I'd also been the only member who had supported and reached out to them, cautioning the commission to heed their message. I still believe it was ACT-UP who spurred the creation of the medications used today to combat HIV/AIDS.

Stirred by these memories during that first day at the CDC meeting, I asked officials if we, the African American participants, should now form BLACK-UP.

That evening, I met in the hotel bar with a number of other AIDS activists, including Debra Fraser-Howze, chair of the Black Leadership Commission on AIDS; Pernessa Seele, from Balm in Gilead; Reverend Edwin Saunders from the Metropolitan Interdenominational Church in Nashville, Tennessee; Reverend Yvette Flunder, a minister from the United Church of Christ in San Francisco; and Alexander Robinson from the National Task Force on AIDS prevention in San Francisco. Why were we getting these damning statistics only now? Could we trust the CDC? Should we take action?

"Let's put out a manifesto," I said.

We worked on our statement until three that morning, choosing Reverend Flunder to voice our concerns at the next session. At seven-thirty in the morning, I arrived to place a copy of our manifesto on each chair. When Flunder still hadn't shown up, people said, "Doc, you take over." I told the assembled CDC staff that we did not want to proceed with the scheduled sessions until we got some solid proposals from the CDC for action against the AIDS disaster in our community.

I also read aloud our press release-manifesto: "[We] are outraged at the nonresponse that the federal agency has had to its own HIV data that clearly represents a national emergency in the black community." I ended with a personal statement: "This is a national public disaster, a national health disaster. Our national response is a travesty that could be perceived as intentional, even genocidal." I demanded that Claire Broome, acting CDC director, and Helen Gayle immediately join the meeting. Emboldened by memories of the 1960s when I had taken part in the occupation of buildings, I said that we demanded a meaningful response from the CDC; that otherwise we were ready to go out and blockade Peachtree Street and maybe more.

Broome and Gayle became cooperative and suggested we propose CDC action. Unfortunately, they were on their way to Washington, DC, to testify the following day before the House Committee on Appropriations in defense of CDC's budget. As she was leaving, Gayle pulled me aside and whispered that it wasn't productive to publicly criticize the CDC and that the policy makers who counted were on Capitol Hill. That afternoon I left Atlanta and flew to Washington to meet with the legislative aides of Democratic House committee members, including Louis Stokes, Nancy Pelosi, and Maxine Waters. I delivered a copy of our manifesto demands to Congressman Stokes's assistant, who had known me for many years as a member of the congressman's brain trust.

The next morning the committee hearing room was almost full, and I took a seat near the back. From the witness table, Broome highlighted President Clinton's stated goal of eliminating minority health disparities by 2010. When pressed by Stokes to confirm that AIDS had reached—based on the CDC's own data—disaster proportions in the United States, Broome responded, "I think that it is a very serious crisis for the African American community...." She had been caught off guard by the passion of the committee members who knew our demands.

On April 29, prior to a vote in the House of Representatives on needle exchange, I attended a meeting of the Health Brain Trust of the Black Caucus headed by Congressman Stokes and including Congresswoman Waters as well as a number of minority AIDS leaders, including Cornelius Baker of the National Association of People with AIDS and Miquelina Maldonado of the National Minority AIDS Council. My recommendation to the group was that carefully monitored exchange programs be implemented because they could prevent HIV infection; and that if properly administered, they could lower drug abuse. The key, I said, was that government should be actively involved through funding and oversight.

Later that day, the House voted 287 to 140 to bar federal money for needle exchange programs. Members of the Congressional Black Caucus predicted that lives would be lost and called for the resignation of drug czar Barry McCaffrey who claimed that needle exchange programs jeopardized the Clinton administration's war on drugs. The issue still remained divisive in the black community. Harlem Congressman Charles Rangel labeled needle exchange "subsidized addiction and death."

(Despite my changed position on the issue, we never distributed needles at ARTC. While we accompanied needle exchange workers in a van to test for HIV, I was reluctant to be directly involved with needle exchange since we received funds from the federal government, which remained opposed to the idea.)

On May 17, just a few weeks after the vote, Congresswoman Waters, then chair of the Congressional Black Caucus, held a meeting at my suggestion in the basement of the Capitol of about sixty black AIDS workers from across the country. She listened all afternoon as they expressed their disappointment and desperation. They had been drowned out in the public debate by gay white organizations that had greater resources to engage the media, organize support, and thus to compete for federal funds. (Bronx Democratic State Senator Israel Ruiz had correctly stated that "gay groups are more vocal, more organized, and have more access to the power brokers.")

"Unequivocally, the African American community is facing a 'state of emergency' in the face of HIV/AIDS," I told the black AIDS workers. "[Based] on every epidemiological measure in common use, when compared to the four other federally recognized racial/ethnic groups (White, Asian/Pacific Islander, Native American/Alaskan Native, Hispanic), African Americans have the highest rates of prevalent HIV infection, the highest mortality rates, and the highest number of productive years lost." I added that in New York City, African Americans represented 46 percent of AIDS cases as compared to 28 percent for non-Hispanic whites, and that the figures were even more astounding for cities like Baltimore, where African Americans accounted for 84 percent. I demanded that resources be provided by Secretary Donna Shalala from emergency funds of the Department of Health and Human Services. "One has only to look at the statistics...to know this money ought to be following the epidemic. It has not."

Four days later, Maxine Waters wrote to Secretary Shalala imploring her to declare a state of emergency in black America. She pointed out that a formal declaration would give the secretary the legal power to take necessary action. There was no response to Waters's letter. Instead, Shalala consulted with Surgeon General David Satcher who, while disappointed in Clinton's decision against needle exchange funding, realized that Clinton was a pragmatist who sought to accomplish the broadest possible agenda. In addition, Satcher was uncomfortable with the term public health "emergency," since the scientific definition implied an acute, containable, and short-term set of conditions. He did not want to give the impression that the epidemic of AIDS in black America could be readily isolated and quickly repaired. Rather, he believed that "AIDS, and the related epidemics of crack cocaine and heroin, had to be understood more broadly in relationship to housing, neighborhood, family, poverty, and community." So Satcher advised Shalala to turn from a statement of a public health emergency to ways to provide funds for treatment, prevention, and education in minority communities.

Meanwhile, pressure on the government to take action was building. On June 29, 1998, theNew York Times published a front-page story headlined the "Epidemic of Silence: A special report; Eyes Shut, Black America Is Being Ravaged by AIDS." The article stated that AIDS had become the de facto largest killer of young black adults, adding that civil rights organizations had, for the most part, still not spoken out on the issue—neither the NAACP nor the Urban League had put AIDS on the agenda for their annual conventions. A spokesman for the Urban League responded that AIDS was "outside our traditional purview," but in July, Julian Bond, chair of the NAACP, did tell a gathering of thirty-five hundred members that "AIDS has become a black epidemic."

As I was having breakfast at home one morning in July, Helen Gayle called to say that because Shalala and Satcher thought that public health "emergencies" were "one-act plays," they preferred to describe AIDS in the black community as a "crisis."

"Well," I said, "if that's the best we can do, it's fine with me as long as we call attention to the problem."

I immediately called Maxine Waters. "No, Beny," she said, "don't you dare. You go after this, and don't you back down for one minute. They're going to ask you to capitulate, but don't you capitulate; don't bend one iota."

"Yes, maam," I answered. "Don't you worry. I won't."

In September, Shalala addressed, in a taped feed, the Congressional Black Caucus's legislative conference, an audience of some fifteen hundred people that included civil rights hero Rosa Parks. Sidestepping mention of a public health emergency, which everyone knew disproportionately affected the black community, Shalala referred instead to "a crisis for all Americans."

In ongoing negotiations, Stokes and Waters insisted the government guarantee a specific amount of funds to black communities, while the government insisted the funds be accessed through existing programs. The internal debate finally subsided when officials felt they no longer could oppose Waters and the Congressional Black Caucus "without being seen as callous, or perhaps even racist," Jacob Levenson observed in *The Secret Epidemic: The Story of AIDS in Black America*.

On October 28, I sat in the front row of the White House briefing room as President Clinton, flanked by a group that included Waters, Stokes, Satcher, and Shalala, stood at the podium and spoke calmly. With the Monica Lewinsky scandal at its boiling point, the president placed the power of his office at the service of AIDS victims: "Like other epidemics before it, AIDS is now hitting hardest where knowledge about the disease is scarce and poverty is high." Characteristically biting his lip when thoughtful, he added, "In other words, as so often happens, it is picking on the most vulnerable among us." Declaring a state of escalating crisis, Clinton promised to fund $156 million to minority AIDS programs. "This milestone today signifies more than a new push against HIV/AIDS," Shalala commented. "It signifies that when it really counts, Washington can pull together to respond to the real needs of real people. It signifies that we have a creative, responsive federal government. It signifies that democracy works—that a devoted group of lawmakers, community leaders, and activists can join forces, raise their voices, demand action, and hold our feet to the fire."

Clinton's Minority AIDS Initiative provided grants for HIV/AIDS prevention, education, and treatment programs serving minority communities. It has expanded considerably since its inception, from a total of $156 million in fiscal year 1999 to approximately $367 million in fiscal 2011.

Finally, at long last, the black community woke up and began to own the problem.

"Prominent black organizations like the National Association for the Advancement of Colored People and traditionally black churches have overcome their reluctance to take on the issue, recognizing that the illness in the last decade has claimed more and more of their own," the *Times* wrote in 1999.

Today I chair the board of Bridging Access to Care (formerly the Brooklyn Aids Task Force) and am chairman emeritus of the National Minority AIDS Council, having served from 1988 to 1993 and again from 1999 to the present. I received the council's lifetime achievement award, presented by Surgeon General Satcher at the National Press Club in Washington in 2000. After helping to found the National Black Leadership Commission on AIDS in 1987, I resigned as its first vice president in 2012, proud to have served with the chair Dr. Calvin O. Butts III, senior pastor of the Abyssinian Baptist Church in Manhattan and president of the State University of New York's College at Old Westbury.

I was profoundly moved when the pioneering and eminent drug abuse researcher Dr. Mary Jeanne Kreek of Rockefeller University commented recently that I "courageously represented a community that was still in triple jeopardy—you are an addict, you have AIDS, and you are gay." In some ways, I was an unlikely advocate.

"For a long time you were homophobic," my daughter Jeanine recalled. "Before HIV arrived, you weren't on that boat. A black man in America? They think gay behavior is weird. But you came to realize the humanity of HIV. You compared intravenous drug users to this other group of outsiders. When it meant that you could help, you changed. You have a healthy underdog syndrome. In the 1980s, you even said to me, 'You need to get involved in AIDS.'"

"Why?" I asked.

"You are really good with people, and they need a lot of help."

As a coda and as an example of how events in life tend to come full circle, my hometown of Williamson, West Virginia, gained notoriety of sorts in the wake of an AIDS incident that made national news. In July 1987, a young, gay white man named Mike Sisco diagnosed with HIV/AIDS returned to Williamson to stay with his family. When Sisco took a dip in the town's public swimming pool, residents fled, and the pool was closed by the city.

Oprah Winfrey pursued the story in Williamson and later televised an hour-long town hall meeting on her show. Sisco was interviewed, and local residents expressed their feelings about AIDS and homosexuality with great vehemence. Even some of Sisco's own relatives shunned him—a "No Trespassing" sign was installed on a family member's lawn.

Later, in September 2010, Winfrey returned to Williamson for a follow-up program, during which several residents apologized to Sisco's sisters (he had died in 1994) for their earlier hateful remarks and lack of compassion. Others, however, said their opinions about the disease and those who suffered from it hadn't changed.

Chapter Nine

Beginnings

―❦―

This was the culture from which I sprang.

Richard Wright, *Black Boy*

I remember my childhood vividly. But to the outside world, I and others like me were invisible, plain and simple. News articles, town documents, historical reports, and club and church notices from the period almost entirely ignore the lives of the African American population. You won't find our story anywhere.

From earliest childhood, I wanted to become a doctor. My father, owner of a funeral home, was friends with all the doctors, and everyone respected them. Even the other kids admired them—we used to throw rocks at cats and dogs, but never at the doctors' animals. I was so taken with the profession that my brother and I would play car wreck just so I could be the doctor. He took the role of funeral director. As it turned out, my brother eventually became a funeral director and I a doctor.

My childhood in Williamson, West Virginia, was an incredibly happy one. I was born upstairs above the Primm Brothers funeral home on May 21, 1928. I have great memories of playing basketball with my brother in our yard, where we nailed a bushel basket to a board and propped it up against the side of the funeral parlor. We had a small rubber ball, not a real basketball, about the size of a soccer ball, and we used that to play with the kids in the neighborhood. At the age of eleven, I would hang out at the school gym where the coach took a liking to me because he liked my mother (the principal). He even made me team manager. I practiced every day, staying late, and learned to keep score. A high point was when the coach included me on out-of-town trips. There were many games, as each hamlet had a black high school and a white high school, each with its own team. (We played only black schools.)

Outside of basketball, the centers of my life were school and my family—mother, father, brother, cousin Dorothy who lived with us, and an orphan named Thomas Adams, who had been adopted by my parents. He later moved to New York and worked for the post office. Soon after my birth, mother got a job teaching in a one-room, all black school in nearby Sprigg, West Virginia, and later in Aflax, Kentucky, which is also close to Williamson, just across the Tug River. I was beyond the babysitter's control by the age of three, so mother took me to school with her. While she taught grades one to six, the sixth graders would take charge of me in the back of the room. If I misbehaved, mother would bring me to the front. So I began school at the age of three.

Probably through my father's political involvement, my mother found better jobs following a Democratic victory in the election of 1932. She was soon promoted to a two-room schoolhouse in the county seat and then became principal of the elementary school, located in Williamson's all-black Liberty High School building. I entered first grade, then skipped to second, then again to third where I stayed for half a year before moving to the fourth grade. At the age of eleven in the eighth grade, I went to a white school to take an exam, scoring the highest in the county for knowing the most about West Virginia history, and was awarded the Golden Horse Shoe and a trip to meet the governor in Charleston, which made everyone in the family extremely proud.

My mother did not allow me to make friends with most boys, even though they mainly played cowboys and Indians. She believed that they would teach me bad habits. She declared out-of-bounds the black business section where there were four or five gambling houses. Fittingly, my best friend was a church deacon's son. Mother was protective and dominant, and we all looked up to her for advice. Her influence on the development of my character cannot be overemphasized—her strict guidance and constant care provided a solid foundation.

My father and uncle's successful funeral home business catered to the black community (though a white soldier was brought there). Primm Brothers gave us financial security, so that our family enjoyed a measure of stability that was hard to come by in the segregated south.

My father was a principled man, with a clear sense of what was just. His defense of miners and voters impressed upon me the importance of defending the rights of those less privileged. Because of his political involvement, my father had experienced his share of trouble with white racists. He often worried about my safety, indicating "that's a Klansman" about someone. He knew whom to avoid, and I stayed away. He carried a gun in a holster and another, a two-shot Dillinger pistol, in a sock. As a child, I sometimes had the impression that I was safer indoors among the dead than outdoors among the living.

The only black folk more revered in town than my parents were the doctor and dentist. This sense of solidity and the easy familiarity of a small town enabled me, I believe, to steer my own course with assurance in later life.

My father, George Primm, was born in 1896 on a farm on Reed Island, Virginia. His father, also named George, was born there either as a slave or soon after the Civil War as a free man; but like many African Americans during the period of slavery and afterward, he had little knowledge of his forebears. At the age of twelve, my father was hired to work on the railroad, one of the few white-owned businesses where blacks could find jobs. His was to clean out the "honey buckets" slung underneath the passenger cars to catch bodily wastes.

My mother, Willie Henrietta Martin, was born in 1897 in Oliver Springs, Tennessee, the daughter of Benjamin Jay Martin, who was born into slavery in 1864. During Reconstruction, he became a United Methodist minister. I am his namesake.

My father met my mother during World War I at a United Methodist Church in Roanoke, Virginia. During the war, my father was drafted into the segregated army and stationed at the Aberdeen Proving Grounds in Maryland. He was honorably discharged in 1918 at the end of the war, and my mother and father married soon after. The young couple took jobs as a maid and butler for a white family in Wheeling, West Virginia.

After about a year, my father enrolled in the Cincinnati College of Embalming in Cincinnati, Ohio, not far from Wheeling. It was difficult then for black men to get loans from banks unless they held government jobs, but my father's brother Frank was a combat veteran and worked as a janitor for the post office in Williamson. In this way, he was able to secure a loan, which he used to help pay for my father's education and to open a funeral home in Williamson, in the southwestern corner of the state in Mingo County, a stone's throw from Kentucky.

In 1921, as my father and Uncle Frank were establishing their business, the area was in bitter conflict over the question of unionization. Shortly after opening his business, my father started a burial association with the United Mine Workers (UMW) to help defray the cost of interring coal miners killed in mine accidents. He befriended John L. Lewis, the legendary president of the UMW, whom I remember joining my father at our kitchen table to share a glass or two of moonshine. They presented quite a picture that made a lasting impression on me: a black working-class man sitting beside Lewis, a large, white man with scary, dominant eyebrows and a large shock of hair.

The mines offered a different social dynamic than the rest of Williamson. They were integrated, and the miners had to depend on each other to save their own lives, which led to a form of mutual dependency between blacks and whites. I know this since several of my uncles worked in the mines for a number of years. It was the only employment available.

Coal had come to dominate life in Williamson. As the union gained strength, the resistance of the coal companies accelerated. In May 1920, the violence that erupted in the town of Matewan, just a few miles from Williamson, would lead to an iconic struggle in the history of American labor relations. Concerned about union efforts, the Stone Mountain Coal Company hired detectives from the Baldwin-Felts Agency to suppress UMW activity. On the morning of May 19, several were sent to evict mineworkers and their families from company-owned housing. When the local sheriff objected, shooting broke out, and ten men, including seven detectives, were killed. The "Matewan Massacre" ignited a war between the miners and the coal companies in Mingo County that culminated in the largest armed uprising since the Civil War and lasted almost a year. It ended only when the army was called in by President Woodrow Wilson.

In the short term, the battle was an overwhelming victory for management. It was not until 1935—in the middle of the Great Depression and at the beginning of prolabor New Deal legislation under President Roosevelt—that the UMW was fully organized in Mingo.

While the mines were now integrated, aboveground Williamson was largely segregated, with separate black and white neighborhoods that in some cases abutted. There were separate schools, hospital wards, and seating in movie theaters. My close childhood friend Travis Fulghan remembers going to "the Cinderella movie theater, watching serials of Johnny Mack Brown, Tex Ritter, and Gene Autry, sitting in the balcony," the section for black folks. But Travis also reminded me that neither the railroad nor the bus station had separate waiting areas for blacks and whites. Historian Joe William Trotter Jr. summed it up: "Blacks in the Mountain State faced fewer incidents of mob violence, less labor exploitation and...fewer constraints on their civil rights than their southernmost kinsmen. Compared to the urban north, however, blacks in the coalfields confronted a legal system of racial segregation. They also faced greater injustice before the law and a more hostile social environment, including a lynching atmosphere, when they allegedly violated segregationist norms."

This story of my father illustrates the racist environment. The funeral parlors were at the back of our clapboard house on Third Avenue in the center of Williamson, just across the street from the tracks where railroad cars loaded with coal passed endlessly. Owning more vehicles than any other black man in Williamson or Mingo County, my father used his two cars and hearse to get voters to the polls on election days and distributed pints of whisky that Lewis provided to influence voters.

The mere act of voting in those days often required a certain amount of courage. In the 1932 elections for Williamson's mayor and police chief,

Walter Murany, a brakeman on the Norfolk and Western Railroad, was promising a bottle of whiskey and five dollars to anyone who would vote for the Republican. On line to vote, my father would have nothing to do with him. "He didn't take nothin' from nobody," remembers Alvin Leonard, whose dad was a close friend of my father. "Then a peckerwood said, 'You can't vote Democratic,' and pointed a gun at him. But Primm rolled up his shirt to show the pistol that was tucked in his belt. He didn't take no bullshit."

Two years later, Sheriff W. E. Hatfield of the infamous Hatfield clan (a name synonymous with long-standing, violent feuds) arrested my father and kept him in jail on trumped-up charges until after election day. He had blocked my father's vote and engaged in a flagrant display of white power. He lost the election anyway.

Blacks were simply not included in the official narrative of Williamson. In front of the 1933 Williamson Chamber of Commerce building (for years the only structure in the world made entirely of coal) stands a broken fountain with a statue of Chief Logan of the Mingo tribe, after whom the county is named. His skin is painted unnaturally red. Below the statue is a plaque bearing the inscription: "Such was my love for the whites that my countrymen pointed as they passed and said, 'Logan is a friend of white men.'" Nowhere is there any mention of black people. It still seems strange to me that at the time the statue was erected, Williamson's population of about 9,500 was 10 percent black. We had been erased from the town's history.

Just as I entered my teens, my family undertook a dramatic change. My mother was absorbed in the problem of giving her children a better education than the one readily available in West Virginia. Meanwhile, hundreds of thousands of blacks were leaving the South in the mass exodus that would come to be called the Great Migration.

Isabel Wilkerson describes the Great Migration in her prize-winning history, *The Warmth of Other Suns*: "Over the course of six decades...some six million black southerners left the land of their forefathers and fanned out across the country for an uncertain existence in nearly every other corner of America. The Great Migration would become a turning point in history. It would transform urban America and recast the social and political order of every city it touched." Blacks traveled northward to New York, Chicago, Philadelphia, and scores of other cities. In the 1930s alone, almost half a million left the South to better their lives economically and to escape the violently harsh codes of segregation. Their actions "were both universal and distinctly American," Wilkerson observes. "Their migration was a response to an economic and social structure not of their making. They did what humans have done for centuries when life became untenable...They left." The life chances of the children "were altered because a parent or grandparent had made the hard decision to leave."

One tributary of the Great Migration took people from West Virginia to Washington, Philadelphia, and New York. Another followed the tracks of the Norfolk and Western Railroad north to Cincinnati and Columbus, Ohio, and surrounding cities. I had previously traveled with my family to Washington, DC, and Niagara Falls, and we had visited New York City, where my mother's sister, Sadie, lived, for the 1939 World's Fair. My parents also learned about life in the north by subscribing to black newspapers such as the *Chicago Defender*, *Pittsburgh Courier*, and *Amsterdam News*.

My mother had an additional reason for leaving West Virginia; my father's philandering embarrassed her in the gossip of the small town. But most important, she believed that her children should attend an integrated school.

I was sad and anxious about leaving the only home I had known and loved. New York seemed like a foreign country. But I was eager to see my older brother who had been sent to New York by my mother to attend school; in any case, there was no arguing with Mother once her mind was made up.

So in September 1941, my mother, cousin Dorothy, and I, along with a jumble of suitcases and boxes, piled into my mother's new Chevrolet and left Williamson for good. Mother had prepared fried chicken and rolls for the trip. We couldn't stop at any restaurant or motel. As there were no rest stops for black people, we had to relieve ourselves at the side of the road.

It wasn't until we had passed through Baltimore and crossed the Mason Dixon line into New Castle, Delaware, that we could stop. There were a number of Howard Johnson restaurants along the highway, and we could finally get something to eat and use the restroom. After driving straight through for more than twelve hours, we arrived in New York City.

Chapter Ten

Hoop Dreams

——— ⌗ ———

I grew up in the Bronx. The Bronx teaches you to survive.

Wesley Snipes

In the early 1940s, the Dunbar Apartments on West 150th Street was one of the most fashionable addresses in Harlem. W. E. B. Du Bois, Paul Robeson, Bill Bojangles Robinson, and A. Philip Randolph had all lived there. Playwright John Henry Redwood described the Harlem of that period as "brimming with great energy. We are ten years removed from the end of Prohibition; we are in the war years. African American soldiers are chomping at the bit to prove themselves again as good citizens by waiting to fight for the Democracy they share very little in. We are just coming out of the Harlem Renaissance. It's the Harlem...of Duke Ellington and Count Basie and all of these giants in music and literature."

Looking back, I find it extraordinary that upon our arrival in New York in 1941, my family stayed with my Aunt Sadie and Uncle Shearl Paige at the Dunbar. What a Harlem beginning!

My uncle had been wounded while serving in World War I in the 369th Infantry Division, the "Harlem Hell Fighters," and subsequently worked for the US Postal Service as a truck driver. This mirrored the experience of many black men who found jobs and economic stability after military service. They could fairly easily get a government job— at the Post Office, the Veterans Administration, or in VA hospitals—which, in turn, enabled them to borrow money from a bank and secure a mortgage. In contrast, many blacks who weren't veterans, even college graduates, could find work only as red caps, bellhops, and pullman porters. My uncle had been fortunate enough to afford the Dunbar.

After a few months with our relatives, my mother purchased a house at 1624 Sedgwick Avenue at 176th Street in the Bronx for $8,000. Moving into the main floor, she sublet the apartment above and the basement below. (One of the later tenants in the basement apartment was a family with a young girl who would grow up to become the actress, singer, and dancer Chita Rivera.) The house was attached to another house on a tree-lined block on a secluded hillside fronted by vacant lots. I played sandlot football on the fields below where, today, vehicles on the Major Deegan speed by endlessly. I could walk down through empty fields to the East River, and there were woods behind the house.

Though much has changed, the old Tudor-style house above the Major Deegan remains the same. The hole on the left side of the roof is still there. The current tenant sits outside on the cement porch watching the world go by, just as my mother did. A boy coming home from school climbs the twenty steps to the front porch, as I did. Gloria Primm Brown, my cousin, remembers that we "always had a lot of people there, students from time to time, even some young women. It was a safe haven for women in the city."

As time passed, I realized that my mother had landed us in the midst of African American culture and history in the making. When we moved to Sedgwick Avenue, about seven families, all black, lived on our block below University Heights. All the houses were in the same Tudor style and built at about the same time. George Gainsford, the manager of Sugar Ray Robinson, lived next door. Sugar Ray would appear behind the wheel of his Pink Cadillac convertible on visits. Playing on the stoop, I'd speak to him. In fact, my first job during my high school years was boxing mail at the main post office. George Gainsford made a couple of phone calls on my behalf, and I was hired. I made $3.50 an hour, which enabled me (in 1944) to buy my first car, the first in a long line of cars. It was a '31

Chevrolet Phaeton. I think I paid fifty-five dollars for it. That was big money in those days. Families sustained themselves with that kind of money.

Dr. Harold Ellis, an eminent psychiatrist, was a resident on the block as well and a few houses down lived Hubert Fauntleroy Julian, called the Black Eagle, a pilot who tried to fly solo across the ocean like Lindberg. Another of his efforts is memorable. On July 4, 1924, he took off in a hydroplane from the Harlem River, hoping to make the first solo flight to Africa. Five minutes into the trip, the *Ethiopia I* lost its right pontoon and crashed into Flushing Bay. Fortunately, Julian survived and continued his flying career.

Then, just a few blocks away was an address that would later become important. "Hip-hop was born in the West Bronx. Not the South Bronx, not Harlem and most definitely not Queens. Just ask anybody at 1520 Sedgwick Avenue [built in 1967]—an otherwise unre-markable high-rise just north of the Cross Bronx and hard along the Major Deegan," wrote David Gonzalez in theNew York Times. "'This is where it came from,' said Clive Campbell, pointing to the building's first-floor community room. 'This is it. The culture started here and went around the world. But this is where it came from. Not anyplace else.' O.K., Mr. Campbell is not just anybody—he is the alpha D.J. of hip-hop. As D.J. Kool Herc, he presided over the turntables at parties in that community room in 1973 that spilled into nearby parks before turning into a global assault."

D.J. Kool Herc later wondered, "Who would have thought that a place like 1520 Sedgwick Avenue, our own little Bethlehem, would become the birthplace of hip hop and would make history?"

The life of my family came together a bit more in early 1942 when my father moved into our house on Sedgwick. He had sold his mortuary business in West Virginia but couldn't get licensure reciprocity in New York and was reluctant to take the qualifying exam. As a World War I veteran, he found a job at the Brooklyn Navy Yard as a night watchman and also drove for a taxi company where he became active in trying to start a union. Sadly, though, the respect and status that he had enjoyed in the black community of Williamson eluded him in New York, and consequently he always seemed a little bit out of place.

With rental income and my father's income, my mother, who had retired as a teacher and school principal, no longer had to work. I count on the memories of my cousin, Gloria Primm Brown, who described my mother as "a large woman, a very forceful woman, the head of the household. She ran everything. She was very astute. Uncle George had to listen to her. He was full of humor and receptive to what we were doing as young people. In his own way, he was a model. He was a person of character who had character of his own. Yet Aunt Willie always prevailed."

She's right. Whatever mother wanted, father wanted too.

Mother believed that my brother and I would be better off if we got an education in integrated schools. That was the main reason she had moved her family to New York. Still, she had distinct paths in mind for my brother Gerome and me. Though he probably could have done well in academics, my mother directed Gerome into vocational training because he was good with his hands. He had preceded my mother and me to New York and graduated from a vocational school as class valedictorian; he had then learned printing before being drafted into the army in 1943.

This period of my life, adolescence through high school and into college, was turbulent. It was a long transition from Williamson, and I struggled to find my footing. Which high school I should attend was the first question. To be accepted at the city's best schools, Bronx High School of Science or Stuyvesant High, students had to take an entrance exam. But by the time we had arrived in New York, the deadline had passed. My brother had always looked out for me, and his teachers told him that I should go to Dewitt Clinton High School. (Dewitt Clinton was founded in 1897 and moved to its current location in the Bedford Park section of the Bronx in 1929. In the 1930s, it was said to be the largest high school in the world.) My brother helped arrange things for me; in September 1941, I entered Clinton, where about five thousand boys were enrolled. What a contrast from my previous school in West Virginia with a total of two hundred students overall and about twenty to thirty in my grade. Clinton was also the biggest building I had ever entered, almost a third of a mile around one floor. You can imagine what it was like walking from one class to another. I was traumatized by its sheer size.

It was also a form of culture shock going to school for the first time with white kids. The school was about 85 percent Jewish; 10 percent Irish, Italian, and Latino; and just 5 percent black. I was very interested in basketball, but if a student wasn't Jewish or Irish, he didn't make the team unless he was truly exceptional. This angered me because I could shoot really well, but I didn't express my anger. It may also have been that I was too short—about five feet eight.

Though intimidated by the basketball program, I still went to practices. Not only did the coach let me hang out, but he took a liking to me so that I became the assistant manager my first year and continued for three years. It was a thrill to be a manager of the Clinton team, especially in 1943 when we played at Madison Square Garden. I was allowed to keep score. (Dolph Schayes—later an NBA star and coach—was in my year and on the team.) When I recently returned to the school, I saw two photographs of the team in which I am standing proudly with the group.

Every afternoon when school ended, I took the subway from Dewitt Clinton in the Bronx to Saint Mark's Church in Harlem. (It cost about ten cents to make the trip from the Bronx to Manhattan and then back to the Bronx by subway and trolley in those days.) I would climb a long flight of steps to the gym on the top floor of the church, where it was always hot. I was in that church every day throughout my high school years, playing basketball. I made the church team as a guard at age fourteen because many of the older guys had enlisted or been drafted in the army.

The teams that we played were primarily from black churches in Harlem, all of which had basketball programs and a league. We also played some Catholic schools, the Grand Street Boys, and the Police Athletic League (PAL). The YMCA had a black league and a white league—always the racial divide.

But prejudice was not confined to the basketball court. There was blatant racism throughout the city. When I arrived in New York, certain restaurants, such as Bickford's, restricted blacks. (The chain did not end its discrimination in Baltimore until 1960.) There was also blatant racism in school. I remember my American history teacher (a Miss Choosy—her real name) haranguing me: "You're never going to Yale, you're going to jail." Years later, when I returned to Dewitt Clinton in my army uniform during the Korean War to pick up a document, I met her in the registrar's office. "Hi Miss Choosy," I said.

She asked, "Who are you?"

"I am Lieutenant Primm."

"You're a lieutenant in the army paratroopers? No wonder we are losing the war."

I will never forget that.

Teased by other boys for wearing knickers, expected in my family until you were sixteen, I got it from both sides. Black kids tried to take my carfare, but they did that only once. The next time I fought back.

Through the churches, I befriended people who, like me, were part of the second-generation black middle class. In those days, Saint Mark's United Methodist Church, the Abyssinian Baptist Church, and Saint Philip's Episcopal Church were the center of our social life. As Dewitt Clinton was an all-boys school, I met girls through the churches. Still, the girls I knew at Saint Mark's wouldn't date me because I wasn't fair-skinned enough. In addition, I was an outsider who had migrated to the city, while most members of the church were New York-born. So there were parties that I wasn't invited to. But I never openly expressed anger or resentment.

The color and class system pervaded the high school, though there were elements of my family background that opened doors for me. The emphasis on education in my family and the fact that my mother, and even her father, had attended college oriented me toward the educated black middle class. The father of one friend, for instance, was Hubert T. Delany, one of the first appointed black judges in New York City. I was friendly with the children of physicians and other professionals whose families lived in the best apartment buildings in Harlem: Sugar Hill, 409 Edgecombe Avenue, and the Roger Morris. One of my best friends and a high school classmate, as mentioned earlier in discussing Martha's Vineyard, was Preston Powell, an adopted son of the late Congressman Adam Clayton Powell.

I was well known in University Heights because I delivered medicine for a pharmacy and, as mentioned, our home was just below the Heights, a Jewish area. One of my Jewish friends there invited me to my first Seder. I even became a member of a club called The Golden Bears, part of the Young Men's Hebrew Association, and played on the Golden Bears basketball team. I was the only black. When my friends and I sneaked into the movies and were caught by managers, I was kicked out probably because I was black. Then the other boys would buy a ticket for me, and I would open the doors for them to get in.

Clinton was academically difficult, and I never really adjusted to it. In Williamson, I had gotten A's effortlessly. But the relationship between teachers and parents in New York City was different from that in West Virginia, where mother would have known immediately if I didn't work hard or receive good grades. In my senior year in high school, a letter was sent home saying that I was suspended for sassing a teacher and that I could return to school only after I brought my mother to meet with the principal. I confess to having intercepted that letter, and the school never followed up.

During the summer break of '43, one of my jobs every weekend was to clean the foyer that led from the porch into the house. One day I went instead to play basketball in a park near Yankee stadium. That night my father really challenged me. We'd had some fights before but nothing significant. This was serious. In the past, he had smacked me with a belt; mother had used a switch. But that night he threw a beer bottle at me that smashed against the wall. I said, "You'd better be glad that didn't hit me," to which he responded, "One of us can't live here and has to leave." I said, "It's me."

A few days later at the age of fifteen, I left home against my parents' will. Coincidentally, my Aunt Sadie had a friend who had come to New York from Tennessee with her husband. Because he was philandering, he had argued with his wife, who now wanted to return home. She needed someone to drive her brand new Buick Road Master back to Johnson City, Tennessee. I volunteered and she agreed. I was mature for my age and had been driving cars with my brother's license. (One car I drove belonged to the neighbor next door, which I used to borrow. Her husband was in the army, and I often took her Chevrolet out and put it back. Sometimes I drove it into Harlem.) In any case, I met my Aunt Sadie's friend at the Theresa Hotel on Seventh Avenue and drove her back to Johnson City. I guess my father felt guilty about what had happened because before I left, he slipped a hundred dollar bill into my hand.

As it happened, my Aunt Addie Martin lived in Johnson City, and I was able to live with her for a couple of weeks. I spent my days at a pool-room, gambling with the money my father had given me and with the one hundred dollars I had earned as chauffeur. The adventure continued when my aunt's friend's husband asked if I would drive to Kingsport, Tennessee, located in a wet county where liquor was legal and where a moonshiner would sell it to me. I would then load up the car and drive back to Johnson City, which was located in a dry county. There, a guy named Smitty would sell the booty. I made this trip about two or three times until my aunt got wind of it: "You're going to get into bad trouble. You need to go and stay with your Methodist minister grandfather in Virginia." With that, I left, took the bus, and stayed with my grandparents in Tazewell, Virginia, for a week or two.

From there I returned to my hometown Williamson, where I found a job driving for Robert Hairston, the husband of my Aunt Sinclair, my mother's best friend. In those days, people had many "aunts" and "uncles" who were not actually blood relatives. Hairston, "Uncle Bob," was a marginal gangster—gambling, the numbers, all illegal—and was said to be the richest black man in Mingo County, where having money made you respectable even if the source was shady. I knew that the town was corrupt and that Hairston was cozy with the police. Still, it was my hometown.

That summer, I drove Uncle Bob and Aunt Sinclair to Idlewild Lake in Northwest Michigan, a favorite vacation spot for African Americans from Chicago, Indianapolis, Detroit, Cleveland, and St. Louis. The trunk of Uncle Bob's 1941 Cadillac was full of moonshine and regular liquor, most welcome in Idlewild, a dry area where a bottle of scotch or bourbon was a big deal. After we arrived, I sold a couple of bottles of Uncle Bob's liquor, unbeknownst to him. I never touched a drop myself. Staying in good shape for basketball was a priority, or maybe my guardian angel was a basketball player.

We stayed in Idlewild for about two or three weeks, so I not only met but got to know the fabulous Jones brothers. Their father was a Baptist minister who had come to Chicago from the South and died shortly afterward, leaving a widow and three sons— Edward, George, and McKissack. From a $16,000 life insurance policy, the boys' mother set her sons up in the taxi business. The venture did well, and the eldest brother, Edward, a former Pullman porter, drifted into the numbers racket, an illegal lottery played mostly in poor neighborhoods, in which a bettor attempts to pick a group of digits to match numbers usually decided by the results of horse races. The gambler places his or her bet with a bookie. A runner then carries the money and betting slips between the betting parlors and the headquarters, called a numbers bank or policy bank. Edward started at the bottom, and by the late 30s, the Jones brothers were grossing $10,000 to $15,000 a day. They funneled their cash into legitimate businesses and real estate, purchasing a Ben Franklin department store, a food store, and several apartment buildings on the South Side of Chicago. This was in addition to their villa in France, where their mother, Harriet, lived; a summer estate in Peoria; and a villa just outside Mexico City.

The entire family had chauffeured limos and lived in enormous mansions. Eddie designed and built his own twenty-one-room mansion in Chicago with custom-made French provincial furniture and gold bathroom fixtures. His wife, Lydia, a former beauty queen in the Cotton Club chorus line, wore satin or mink every day. Money propelled them into a social world that otherwise would have been out of reach. Uncle Bob played Georgia Skins cards with them and stayed in their huge house. I remember attending a party at their club, where Nat King Cole's trio performed.

Several years after my encounter with the Jones brothers, they experienced a crisis. In May 1946, Eddie was kidnapped in Chicago by white gangsters. He was released after a few days with adhesive tape over his eyes and cotton stuffed in his ears. His brother George had paid the

$100,000 ransom. Soon after he was released, the brothers retired to Mexico.

Toward the end of August, I drove the Hairstons back to Williamson and from there took a Greyhound bus to New York. My Aunt Sinclair probably had informed my mother of my whereabouts and activities. From then on, I never gave my parents trouble. I also made up with my father, and we became very close. Overall, my experiences that summer, and my assessment of them, convinced me of the path I *didn't* want to follow in life.

In high school, I got caught up with the rabble—if not the worst, not a good bunch either—and my studies slipped as well. When it came time to graduate in June 1944, I had to stay another semester because I had failed New York State's Latin Regents Exam with a score of sixty-two when sixty-five was the minimum required for an academic diploma. I returned in September—only to score sixty-four, which was heartbreaking. So in 1945, I received a general diploma instead of the academic diploma.,

Among the graduates in my high school class were several young men who later became prominent in their fields. They included playwright Neil Simon; New York real estate magnate Lewis Rudin; and songwriter Fred Ebb, who wrote the lyrics both for *Chicago* (which starred Chita Rivera when it first opened on Broadway in 1975) and the Liza Minnelli film *New York, New York*. In the 1944 Dewitt Clinton Yearbook, my goal is "to become an M.D.," and I cite the school's motto: "Sine Labore Nihil" (without labor nothing). My nickname is "Shorty." The picture shows a boy with a half smile, wearing a bow tie, who looks about thirteen years old.

When I visited Dewitt Clinton in 2012 as an eighty-four-year-old doctor and world authority on substance abuse treatment, the principal asked if I would be the commencement speaker. This was most gratifying.

These early years were full of twists and turns. Always struggling to find my footing, my task now was to find a suitable college. My friends were going to Lincoln, Morgan, Howard, Fisk, a few to Clark, some to Wilberforce, and others to the City College of New York. I was set on

NYU but realized that I lacked the grades. Mother leaned toward City College, which was free, but their day program required an average of eighty-five in Regents exams. At this point, certain significant people in my life suggested a different path. Samuel C. Brisbane, my basketball coach at Saint Mark's, and the Reverend Grant Shockley, assistant pastor, both recommended Lincoln University. Brisbane had attended Clinton and graduated as a premed student from Lincoln in 1938. (Brisbane later became an anesthesiologist at Harlem Hospital, and my first job there was in anesthesia with him.) Shockley had also graduated from Lincoln. To top it off, Brisbane arranged a one-hundred–dollar scholarship for me. So from Clinton, I went straight to Lincoln University in Pennsylvania, entering in January 1945, the same year that Dr. Horace Mann Bond, himself an alumnus of Lincoln, was selected as the first African American president of the university.

Located near the town of Oxford in Southern Chester County, Pennsylvania, Lincoln was the first degree-granting, historically black university in America. In 1854, Rev. John Miller Dickey, a Presbyterian minister, and his wife, Sarah Emlen Cresson, a Quaker, founded the Ashmun Institute. In 1866, following the assassination of President Abraham Lincoln, the Ashmun Institute was renamed Lincoln University. Dr. Bond noted in his *Education for Freedom: A History of Lincoln University, Pennsylvania:* "This was the first institution founded anywhere in the world to provide a higher education in the arts and sciences for youth of African descent." Notable alumni included: US Supreme Court Justice Thurgood Marshall; Harlem Renaissance poet Langston Hughes; musical legend Cab Calloway, who attended but left before graduating; the first president of Nigeria, Nnamdi Azikiwe; and the first president of Ghana, Kwame Nkrumah.

Despite high hopes, my stay at Lincoln was short—until March 1946. Many of the older athletes who had gone into the service returned and took their places on the varsity basketball team. I was disappointed to be demoted from the varsity to the junior varsity team, and my studies went poorly. Also, Lincoln was a men's college, and I realized that I wanted to meet women. That May I would turn eighteen. So in March

1946, I left, returning home with the idea of joining the army. Naturally, my mother insisted I work and attend school. I was admitted to the City College night school, where I joined the basketball team and took several courses. But in September 1946, after one semester, I transferred to West Virginia State. Years earlier, Mother had completed her credits during the summer months for a BS there, taking my brother and me along with her from Williamson. On my application, I gave as my home address that of my Aunt Sinclair in Williamson so I could qualify for the lower tuition of a West Virginia resident.

West Virginia State, about eight miles west of Charleston, is located on "land granted to George Washington for his service in the King's Military before the Revolutionary War." Much later, as a slave plantation, it belonged to the Cabbel family. Sam Cabbel married Mary Barnes, one of his slaves, who sold the land to the state after Cabbel's death. The school was established as the West Virginia Colored Institute in 1891 and from then until 1915, "the school provided the equivalent of a high school education, with vocational training and teacher preparation for segregated public schools." In 1929 the State of West Virginia recognized the school as a four-year institution and changed its name to West Virginia State College. During the 1930s and 1940s, it came to be recognized nationally as one of the premier institutions in the education of black students.

Historically black colleges and universities, mainly established by white philanthropists, generally provided religious education and limited training in basic skills. For the most part, these institutions were established during the mid- to late 1800s. After the Civil War, more black colleges and universities were created to provide for the education of the newly freed slaves. As Kenneth E. Redd has written in "Historically Black Colleges and Universities," most were established in the southern states under the auspices of the Freedmen's Bureau, black churches, and white philanthropies. Because most of the teachers and administrators at these institutions were white, they generally sought to teach their students codes of conduct acceptable to white society.

I was happy at West Virginia State. It was like going home. But again, as at Lincoln, basketball presented obstacles. The rules stipulated that a transfer student couldn't play during his first year in attendance. Because of my height, I wouldn't have made the team anyway, and I didn't even try the second year. I did, however, play on the fraternity team. There were great frat teams at West Virginia, and my fraternity, Alpha Phi Alpha, won the championship each year that I played.

I began ROTC training in 1946 at West Virginia State. There was a military tradition in my family. My father had served in World War I; some of my uncles, as mentioned, had also served. My brother Gerome served as well. He had been drafted into the army in 1943 at the age of eighteen. During his first two or three years, he installed electrical wiring, then worked as a stevedore and truck driver. He served most of his time in the South Pacific as a warrant officer, fourth grade, and was promoted to chief warrant officer before leaving the army in 1948. Gerome had earned his rank the hard way, helping to maintain equipment and technical systems. After his discharge, he had a tough time adjusting to civilian life. He drank and almost killed himself in a car accident. Back on his feet, he took college courses, graduating from the McAlister Institute, a mortuary science school in New York City. Our parents then bought a funeral home for him in Mount Vernon, New York, and part ownership of another in the Bronx, both called the Primm Funeral Home. Gerome was successful in the business and became president of the National Funeral Directors Association. In 2003, at the age of seventy-eight, he died. I often wonder how his life might have been different if he had made a career in the army. When I joined ROTC at college, it was on Gerome's advice, which included a not so subtle warning: "If you're in the army and you're not an officer, your ass is grass."

As a cadet, I avoided the draft. Maintaining good standing in ROTC depended on attitude and performance. There was a written test at the end of the junior year for which I studied the night before, passing with a perfect score. The higher-ups doubted the results and made me take the test again. Another perfect score and still they didn't believe me; they thought I had cheated.

Attitude was another matter. Unfortunately, my lip got the better of me. Among the student ROTC officers were guys who had returned from the war somewhat hardened. They could be mean and inclined to insult us, and I wasn't taking it. The problem was that every time we spoke out of turn or didn't do our job as expected, a demerit resulted. I accumulated scores of demerits. To think about it now, I'm surprised I wasn't dismissed, though they did say I'd never make a good soldier. Fortunately, I had the support of Dr. Roscoe Brown, my college phys-ed teacher, who also knew me from pick-up basketball games and from his class in kinesthesiology, the study of movement and joints, where I'd earned an A. Just returned from duty, he was a former Tuskegee Airman, who later became a university professor at the City University of New York and eventually president of Bronx Community College. With support among the ROTC officers, the colonel in charge set aside the accusations of cheating and of my brash attitude. Instead, everything would depend on my performance at summer camp for intensive training between my junior and senior years at Fort Bragg in Fayetteville, North Carolina.

There I was competing with guys from West Virginia State, Hampton, and Howard, as well as with white cadets from the Virginia Military Institute, the Citadel, etc. So when I excelled in all the military drills and was selected as first battalion commander whose privilege it was to lead the troops at the end of the summer in the final parade, I was thrilled. Passing in review before the generals was the highest honor offered to an ROTC cadet. I never will forget it: the dress uniforms, the swords, marching in perfect unison to "The Stars and Stripes Forever."

Following that experience, I grew more responsible and confident. I believe the discipline taught me that following orders was more effective than talking back. I became serious about military science and tactics, learning how to command, how to gain the respect of men, how to create a team. That was the summer I grew up—the summer of 1949.

Returning to West Virginia State in the fall, I became a company commander, the third highest-ranking cadet in our corps. Because four years were required in the ROTC program to receive a commission, I had to spend an extra year in college. During that time, I took courses in the biological sciences and finished as a C-plus, B-minus student. (I began to study seriously only later in medical school.) In May 1950, I graduated with the rank of second lieutenant.

Of particular note during these turbulent college years were the summers of 1947 and 1948. A candidate had to be at least five feet eight, of a certain weight, and with a certain manner of speech to be hired. The only blacks on staff were chambermaids and bellhops—no waiters. I'm speaking of the famed Greenbrier Resort in White Sulphur Springs, West Virginia. Passing muster upon application, I was hired as a bellhop. Thus began an unforgettable introduction to the world of the white upper class in America.

Bellhops were to stand along the white pillars in the lobby until summoned. One day, a kindly gentleman motioned me forward. "My guys and I will be playing golf. Will you bring us drinks when we finish?" Of course, the minute they exited the golf course, I made it my business to be available. The tip for these few services was $100. I was also given a beautiful rep tie that I wore for years. The kindly gentleman turned out to be no less than the millionaire philanthropist Andrew Mellon himself.

That first summer I earned about $2,000, mostly in tips—salaries amounted to only $20 to $30 a week. During my second summer at the Greenbrier, I took a different tack and attempted to form a union. Bellhops were routinely taken off the line to run the elevators for two to three hours, which meant lost tips. My position was that they should hire elevator operators, and I stated that I would refuse to take the elevator shift, hopefully prompting others to do the same, which would amount to a strike.

The day following my announcement, a large staff meeting was called; the hotel manager asked, "Who is this Primm?"

I identified myself.

"You're fired."

About a month later, elevator operators were hired at the resort. So, while that was the end of my Greenbrier career, it was the beginning of my effort to address inequity. I realized how persistent that can be when I returned to White Sulphur Springs twenty years ago for a meeting of the board of Meharry Medical College. There, to my shock, were some of the men who had refused to join me in my bid to form a union— still working as Greenbrier bellhops.

In August, following my graduation from West Virginia State, I was assigned as an artillery officer to the 98th Field Artillery Battalion in the 82nd Airborne Division at Fort Bragg. From that point on, my life changed in ways I could never have imagined.

Chapter Eleven

Turning Points

———— ∞∞∞ ————

There are no "white" or "colored" signs on the foxholes or graveyards of battle.

John F. Kennedy

Following graduation and before heading to Fort Bragg, I returned home to the Bronx for three months. I suppose my parents noticed a change in me, though they never really commented on it. I believe they were simply proud that I had graduated from college. As for me, I was looking ahead. I'd had some airborne training during my final year in college and had decided to join the elite corps of paratroopers.

When I reported for duty in August, the Korean War was already underway. On June 25, soldiers from the North Korean People's Army had stormed across the 38th parallel, the boundary between the Soviet-backed Democratic People's Republic of Korea to the north and the pro-Western Republic of Korea to the south. By July, American troops had entered the war on South Korea's behalf. At Fort Bragg, the shadow of combat loomed.

During the first few months, I went on maneuvers. After about four months, I entered jump school. First came jumps from the 34-foot towers, then from 250-foot towers. Mundane tasks such as packing our own parachutes broke the tension.

My first jump from an airplane—also my first time *in* an airplane—occurred during our fifth week of training. As an officer, I was anchorman and led the stick (the line of men exiting from each door): lean forward, dig in, and push as hard as you can. Communication was restricted to nine verbal commands, each shouted over the roar of the engines and accompanied by a distinctive hand signal from the jumpmaster. To this day I remember the commands: "Get Ready," "Stand Up," "Hook Up," "Check Static Line," "Check Equipment," "Sound Off for Equipment Check," "Stand in the Door," "Ready," "Go!" Obviously, timing was crucial; if we missed the drop zone, we could end up in water or in a tree.

Needless to say, the maneuver was nerve-wracking, especially at the beginning. On about the third jump, a couple of men just froze in the door. In truth, each of the five times I jumped, I was terrified too. After every jump, there would be a couple of men who left the unit and were reassigned to other duties. But everyone who made it through bonded as paratroopers. We all knew that one person's mistake could cost another's life. That created a connection that endured long after I left the service. In fact, it's a feeling I've never forgotten.

Following paratrooper training, I was assigned to the 80th Airborne AA Battalion commanded by then Major Jetty Gates. He had formerly been a member of the 369th Infantry Regiment, called the Harlem Hellfighters by their German foes, a unit in which my brother and uncle had served. Gates took it upon himself to look after me.

Of course, there was down time. I had a car at Fort Bragg and drove to New York City about once a month to shop and go out on the town, usually with several fellows from the base. The drive took nine to ten hours each way, but we felt it was worth it. Ernest Fant, a friend from that time, summed it up: "We left by four on a Friday afternoon to give us enough time to reach the city before the bars closed."

Then, rather abruptly, the fun ended. In the winter of 1951, while driving through a heavy thunderstorm to Durham, North Carolina, my car skidded into a tree. I had been on my way to escort a young lady to a debutante ball, when, about forty miles from Fayetteville in Holly Springs on Route 55, I lost control. Fortunately, a white couple who lived across the street heard the crash and carried me out of the car. I couldn't move and was in terrible pain. They put me to bed for the few hours before the ambulance arrived to take me to the hospital at Fort Bragg. My left leg was a mess: a fractured femur, a compound fracture of the tibia and fibula, and torn lateral and collateral ligaments. I remained in the hospital and in traction for four months before I could move around in a cast, and I was in constant pain.

Amazingly, my date for the ball remained convinced I'd stood her up. She wouldn't believe I was injured and, despite the proof, never even came to visit me in the hospital. But this was a small matter compared to the consequences for my military career.

In the fall of 1952, while in and out of the hospital for physical therapy, I returned to active duty, though I was being processed for retirement based on my disability. Not for another two years was I able to throw the brace away. Still, my left leg continued to bother me, and, in 2001, I finally had to have my knee replaced. Nevertheless, I realized I was lucky. Several of my friends had died in Korea, and the injury prevented me from seeing combat. After the accident, I appeared frequently before the review board for evaluation for retirement. Finally, the board decided that I was two-thirds disabled and should be retired from duty. After another Pentagon review, my level of disability was lowered to one-third and finalized.

One of the most important aspects of my military experience, which shaped me as a person, was that of race. Officially, the federal government had acted against discrimination in the military through an executive order issued by President Harry Truman on July 26, 1948. This purportedly abolished racial discrimination. Truman's order stated: "This policy shall be put into effect as rapidly as possible." But the military hierarchy dragged its feet. Almost a year later, in April 1949, Secretary of the Army Kenneth Claiborne Royall was forced into retirement for failing—and refusing—to take the necessary steps to desegregate the army.

When I arrived at Fort Bragg, all the units were segregated. Whites commanded black units, but blacks could not command white units. Living conditions and barracks were different for whites and blacks.

Ours were wooden, and theirs were brick. There was an exclusive white officers' club and a black officers' club. And while there was resentment among black soldiers, there was never talk of trying to bring change. The rules were strict, and punishment for violating the segregation policies was swift and inhumane. During my stay, one of the black officers at Fort Bragg was caught having a relationship with a white soldier's wife. For that he received a prison sentence of ninety-nine years.

By the fall of 1952, all the services were officially integrated, but racial discrimination was still prevalent. There were black enlisted men, but most of the officer corps was white. After discharge from the hospital, I was assigned to an all-white unit, the 456th Airborne Field Artillery Battalion, which had about four hundred men in it. There I became the first black officer in the 82nd Airborne to command white troops.

Of course, on paper this all looked great. But instead of naming me a battery commander—called for by my rank of first lieutenant—they made me the battalion intelligence officer, which required the rank of major, two ranks above mine. It made no sense. I hadn't been on active duty long enough to achieve the rank of major. But beyond that, the white officers, many of them graduates of military schools such as the Citadel, the Virginia Military Institute, and Texas A&M, remained resentful. The truth is they were steeped in the military tradition of the confederacy. The sergeant in the intelligence division was a redneck and didn't want a black guy in charge. It was as simple and as biased as that.

Furthermore, the brass who gave me the assignment knew just what they were doing. It was common practice to promote black officers to a high rank in order to bust them out of the army. It took only a couple of bad reports to ruin their careers. Black officers who stayed in the service had to be exceptional to get a decent report. Still, I had no choice but to take the job and so remained battalion intelligence officer while being evaluated for permanent disability.

My leg brace didn't stop the white officers from giving me an especially hard time during the hazing ritual known as the prop blast. The prop blast is an honored airborne tradition and represents a traditional "rite of passage" for officers who have served with the parachute forces.

Thirteen paratroopers stationed at Fort Benning, Georgia, started the prop blast in December 1940, naming it after the blast of air that hits jumpers after exiting an aircraft. It included a mock jump, running an obstacle course, and drinking a cocktail of mixed booze out of an artillery shell. I was the only black, and my hazing was worse.

Black soldiers who served their country in the ways that discrimination permitted also had to maneuver past the unwelcoming face of racism off base in the Fayetteville of the 1950s, just seven miles from Fort Bragg. In those days, there was one restaurant for blacks, a couple of drive-ins, and a small area for black businesses. The movie theater required blacks to sit upstairs in the balcony. Still standing today in the center of town is a historic landmark known as the Market House, which served as a slave market before abolition. Slaves were sold under the open, first-floor arcade, while the second floor served as the town hall and general meeting place.

Despite the racism and painful historic landmarks, it has also become clear that the service of blacks in the military, particularly during wartime, gradually fostered integration. Serving side by side, often in dangerous situations, created trust between blacks and whites, and those experiences helped break down prejudice.

In addition to achieving personal maturity as a soldier, able to both follow and give orders, this period also brought me romantic happiness. Prior to the automobile accident, I'd met a pretty, young woman in Fayetteville at a drug store soda fountain and immediately recognized her as a USO junior hostess volunteer from summer camp at Fort Bragg. Her name was Annie Delphine Evans. (Delphine was her preferred name.) Two years my junior, Delphine was finishing her senior year at Fisk University in Nashville, Tennessee, as a music major. When she came home from college to visit her folks, she also stopped to visit me in the hospital. I'd previously asked her for a date, but she was engaged to a dentist and so declined. Her attitude seemed to soften when she saw how badly injured I was.

I was sometimes able to visit her at Fisk. Before long, Delphine and I had fallen in love and decided to get married. The ceremony took place on December 31, 1951, at the Fayetteville home of Colonel James H. Porter who had become a good friend. (He commanded the "Triple Nickels," a unit of black paratroopers who, instead of serving overseas during World War II, fought forest fires at home, as white commanders had "no use" for black jumpers.) The reception was held at the black officers' club on the base. My friends and I must have been an impressive sight dressed in military whites, even though I still wore a waist-high cast, a steel bar through my ankle, and a brace.

Because female students at Fisk were not permitted to marry before graduation, we had to do our best to keep our marriage a secret until Delphine's commencement the following May. In September 1952, she began teaching music and directing the choir at the E. E. Smith High School in Fayetteville, where she had been a student, and we moved into an apartment of our own in town. It seems I was pretty possessive as a young husband. My longtime friend E. J. Smith, who was a house guest in those years, later recalled: "You used to wake me up in the mornings when you'd leave for the base and tell me, 'You can't stay here with Nicey' as you called her. You didn't want a single guy in the house with your new wife."

On September 30, 1953, two months after the end of the Korean War, I was discharged from the army with a medical retirement and one-third of my annual base pay. Eventually, these funds helped pay for my medical education, and I've received the same portion of my base pay of that time ever since.

Looking back, I've realized that fate sets us along paths with surprising destinations. Overcoming my fear and defensive attitude and managing the discrimination I encountered in the army gave me confidence. It transformed me from a smart-ass kid into a man, brought Delphine into my life, and helped pay for medical school. Ironically, the most favorable outcome may have been my forced retirement as a result of the accident. Otherwise, I most likely would have been sent to Korea; and if I had survived, I might have made the army my career. And I'd always had my heart set on becoming a doctor.

Chapter Twelve

Stranger in a Strange Land

---oee---

*...it is healing and refreshing to breathe in air that has known
no taint of slavery for six hundred years, and to come among a
people whose political history is great and fine, and worthy to be
taught in all schools and studied by all races and peoples.*

Mark Twain, *Travel Letters*

I've often been asked how I could have become such a gung-ho soldier
while continuing to dream of practicing medicine. When my father
and brother hunted squirrels and groundhogs in Williamson, I never
joined them because I didn't want to kill. But, like many others, I ration-
alized that in war you must kill the enemy. I remember the adrenalin
rush of leading troops during the summer parade at ROTC camp. A fear
of combat vied with images of leading soldiers into battle. It all seemed
glorious and heroic. For most of my life, I have been an idealist; but during my first years in the army, I became a romantic.

Confined to my hospital bed at Fort Bragg after the automobile accident, I'd spent hours studying *Gray's Anatomy* and physiology books,
focusing more intensely on medical school. But an obstacle I hadn't considered intervened. In 1953, there weren't many medical schools in the
country that would admit a black man.

The vast majority of black medical students were being trained at
Howard University in Washington, DC, and Meharry Medical College

in Nashville, Tennessee. Howard University, perhaps the principal black institution in the country, was named after its founder Major General Oliver Otis Howard, a white Civil War officer who became a leader in promoting higher education for freed slaves. Meharry, the only other black medical school to remain certified into the twentieth century, had begun as Central Tennessee College. It opened its medical department in 1876 and was renamed the Meharry Medical College.

In the North, there was scant opportunity. "A select few of the Ivy League medical schools were admitting 'exceptionally talented' black males," Rudolph Cumberbatch, a black doctor, wrote in his book *Failure Masquerading as Success*. "But there was a quota. At Harvard the quota appeared to me to have been two in the medical school and one in dental school. In my graduating class of 1959, two of us started but only one graduated."

These statistics reflect the society of the times, when medical practice itself in the United States was highly segregated. If a person was black and needed care, he or she went to a certain section in a hospital. Black staff treated mainly black patients, and black doctors didn't have the privileges white doctors enjoyed. Hospitals even separated donated blood by race; there was black blood and white blood.

In 1953, I applied to Meharry but was turned down. I knew my college grades would not gain me admittance to Howard. My dream seemed stalled. But before I was discharged from the army, Alexander Boyd Jordan, an old school friend, had visited me at Fort Bragg. Even as a Regents Scholar and a national champion cross-country runner, his applications to US medical schools had been rejected. Some of his Jewish friends had also been turned down by medical schools in the United States and had gone abroad to study. Appreciating my predicament, Jordan suggested I apply to medical school in Geneva where he had been accepted in 1948. When I said that I feared studies in French would present a serious obstacle, he then proposed Heidelberg University in Germany and Innsbruck University in Austria and guided me through the application process. To my surprise, I was admitted to both. I chose Heidelberg because, as a biological science and German major in college, I had heard praise of the university.

It was interesting to learn that African Americans had been studying abroad for more than a century. I was particularly fascinated by James McCune Smith, who, in the early 1800s after graduating from high school, applied to Columbia University and the Geneva Medical College in New York State but was denied admission to both. With money and assistance from abolitionist benefactors, Smith was admitted to Glasgow University, where he obtained a medical degree in 1837—truly a trailblazer.

As encouraging as these success stories seemed, I still hesitated about medical school abroad. First, studying in a foreign language, even one I was familiar with, seemed problematic; also, Delphine had concerns about a long medical program in Germany, though she didn't want to stand in my way. After long discussions, we agreed that she would remain in Fayetteville, where she was teaching, and join me later once I was settled. My parents expressed confidence in my ability to handle the challenge, particularly my mother who had always encouraged me to become a doctor.

Following my medical discharge from the army on September 30, 1953, my friends threw me a party at Fort Bragg. I was touched by the support of my fellow officers. Toward the end, my tears flowed. I was frightened of the unknown and of pursuing my dream in a totally foreign environment on my own.

On October 5, I headed to New York from Fayetteville to board the Cunard Line's *Queen Mary* for the voyage to France, the first stop on my European journey. When the ship couldn't dock in Manhattan due to a tugboat strike, we passengers were put on a train to embark from Halifax, Nova Scotia, where we went aboard two days later. This was my first experience traveling by ship. After departure, I began to socialize and soon met some bridge players. Here I was well prepared. My mother, an expert, had coached me, and I won nine hundred dollars at bridge while crossing the Atlantic.

After about a week, we docked at Le Havre and I took the boat train to Paris, speaking not a word of French. I couldn't even order a croissant, which turned out to be the least of my worries. When the train arrived at the Gare Saint-Lazare, I searched for bathroom facilities. Someone pointed to a door that opened to a hole in the floor. With a hip-high, steel brace on my leg, I couldn't quite manage and ended up with a soiled new seersucker suit that now needed cleaning. Seeing no recourse, I climbed into a horse trough and cleaned up as best I could. People stared as if I were crazy.

I finally boarded the train to Heidelberg, falling fast asleep in my cabin. When a German conductor came to wake me, his military-like hat provoked images of the Second World War and the racist response to Jesse Owens' athletic feats at the 1936 Olympics in Berlin. Half-dreaming, I almost panicked until I came to my senses.

By the early 1950s, the number of African Americans studying in Germany was small enough to be counted on two hands, and I was now one of them. While Paris had become a mecca for African American writers and musicians, few, if any, chose to travel to Germany. But here I was at Heidelberg University, founded in 1386, Germany's oldest university. During the Nazi period (1933–1945), a large number of staff and students were dismissed on grounds of race or politics. Forced sterilizations took place at the school's surgical clinic as well as at the gynecological hospital. When I arrived, the black students at the medical school included just three Africans, one African American, and now me. For a provincial, black twenty-five-year-old to undertake an extended stay was an act of either stunning naiveté or of blind courage.

The city of Heidelberg was still rebuilding from the war, although there had been relatively little destruction. As a retired military officer, I was able to live in the Hotel Tannhauser in the bachelor officers' quarters. Although US Army headquarters for Europe was based in Heidelberg, soldiers were generally confined to the base, and black soldiers could not go into town, even on furlough. Black students, however, unlike black soldiers, were permitted in town. I wore civilian clothes when I walked in the city, which led to frequent questions from the military police who took me for a soldier gone AWOL. Once enlightened by my identification and my 82nd Airborne Division raincoat, and informed that I was a student and retired army officer, they backed off and saluted me. On trolleys, however, commuting to and from school, I encountered people's glances and comments about the "schwarze"—black man.

In those years, the racist policies of the Nazi years still held sway among many Germans. "The American model of race segregation that still defined much of military life during the 1950s could not but encourage Germans in their conviction that black Americans were not 'true' Americans," Hanna Schissler wrote in *The Miracle Years.* "The comments in 1957 from a white military police officer confirm that such prejudices toward black soldiers still existed despite the almost decade-long effort at desegregation. Observing German women and black soldiers together, he snarled, 'At home in Alabama they would take care of such behavior.'"

With the exception of anatomy and physiology, which included a lot of Latin, the common language of medical students everywhere, I found medical school difficult. But it was for financial reasons that I decided to leave Heidelberg after a year. I was living on eighty dollars a month—just my disability retirement pay—but was entitled to GI bill benefits, which would provide about another $160 a month, enough money to bring Delphine to Europe. The problem was that I could receive funds from the GI bill only if enrolled in school in Holland, Switzerland, France, or Italy. I had no choice but to investigate my options in those countries.

I first went to Zurich and decided to look elsewhere, so on to Basel, where the Schweitzer Deutsch was very difficult. Next came Holland, where everybody spoke English. When I went to the Ministry of Education, the official who interviewed me took a look at the patch on my raincoat sleeve with the insignia of the paratroopers who had landed at Nijmegen, a city in the east of the Netherlands near the German border that had been liberated from the Nazis in September 1944 by British soldiers and the 82nd Airborne Division. He treated me like a war hero, and I was easily admitted to the Radboud University Nijmegen Medical Centre. I sat in class for two or three days but couldn't understand a word of the lectures in Dutch.

Running short on options, I returned to Heidelberg and once again reached out to friends. By now, I had become part of a network of successful black men, partially through my fraternity, Alpha Phi Alpha. Managing to call the states for free (not easy in that era), I contacted Charles Enoch Wilson, who was finishing his medical studies at the University of Geneva.

Wilson had been an executive in a new division Pepsi Cola had created for the African American market but left after a few years, as he had his heart set on becoming a doctor. I arranged to meet Wilson in Geneva. His approach was to go for sympathy. "I'll take you to the registrar, and when I give you a signal to cry, you cry. You've got to do this."

As I sat before the registrar, she reviewed my transcript. Finally, she looked up and said, "I don't know if you can make it here. You had a D in genetics."

"I received the D because I had cut the class six times," I lamely explained, "and the limit was three cuts. I really had an A."

Immediately, Wilson gave the signal and I teared up. "I have to be accepted," I said emotionally. "I don't know any other way." Mademoiselle Grosselin relented. "Well, you have a good background. You were a soldier, a paratrooper. We're going to admit you. I don't know how you're going to make it, but I think you will." I learned later that she had dated a Moor from North Africa and was opposed to the racial prejudice prevalent in the States. I walked out of her office the happiest guy in the world.

When I entered medical school in Geneva in September 1954, there were only about eight black students in the program, seven of whom were from America. One of them was Ralph Waldo Fenderson, who became a close friend. His grandfather had been a minister, a friend of Booker T. Washington and an admirer of Ralph Waldo Emerson.

Meanwhile, Delphine had traveled from Fayetteville to join me. The university placed both of us in a beginning French class. Every night I would memorize the assignment. One day the teacher looked at me and said, "Monsieur, after class I want to see you." I worried. My whole medical school career depended on my proficiency in French. Much to my surprise, she said, "I don't want you to come back anymore." Oh no! I've put all my eggs in this one basket, and she didn't want me back. How was I to learn French? Then she said, "You're going to be OK. I want you to speak every time you have an opportunity. Don't be discouraged. You just don't need to come here."

My wife, on the other hand, was furious because she had to continue. Six or seven months later, I was taking notes half in English, half in

French. I never studied a word of formal French except for the week and a half in that dear woman's class; and despite my earlier concern about medical studies in French, all went surprisingly well.

During our time in Geneva, Delphine and I were treated with a great deal of respect. The residents and faculty were well aware that in America blacks were regarded as second-class citizens, and they were empathetic. Because the UN had begun to expand its offices in Geneva by my third year, there was an influx of Africans. Still, as black Americans we were a curiosity. On the streets people would laugh, point, or even touch us. It was not malicious but an infantile type of behavior. People would bump into signs looking at us, and some would even try to touch my hair. Once, after people kept stopping to stare at Delphine, I grabbed her arm, turned her around, and said, "Here, take a good look at her."

For the most part, we disregarded this ignorance, but there was one serious incident. One afternoon after class, I offered to drive to the market to get cheese and other items for lunch for three or four Jewish friends from the States who were my study partners in school. As I was climbing into my car after picking up the food, a guy on a motorcycle hit my car door. He then called me a dirty nigger in English. Before I knew it, I had struck him in the face and and he had fallen in the street with a bloody nose. I headed home. But no matter how brief, a fight in Switzerland has consequences. People on the scene had taken down my license plate number, and by the time I arrived, the gendarmes were at my door. They arrested me and put me in a cell. Colonel Alfred "Killer" Barnes, a friend in the army in Germany, who happened to be coming to Geneva that day to visit me, testified on my behalf before the judge. After a few hours, I was released on my own recognizance. When the case came up before the court, I had to pay the hospital expenses for my heckler, minus the difference for the damage to my car and my suit.

Apart from this incident, though, my life in Switzerland was wonderful. The Swiss, apart from the curiosity we attracted on the street, were kind and cordial. And I loved the food. At the time, my friend Fenderson was dating a Liberian woman. She was from a well-to-do family and looked out for us. Also, I became friendly with employees who worked at the newly opened UN offices, and there were many diplomatic parties. We sometimes drove into the mountains above Geneva for picnics.

Since I had a car, Fenderson and I traveled to Annecy and Cannes to play roulette and boule at the casino. We crossed the Pyrenees into Spain and visited the Italian Riviera.

Geneva stayed open late at night and through the "Jazz at the Philharmonic" series in New York City, a number of jazz greats came to Geneva, including Dizzy Gillespie, Count Basie, Oscar Peterson, Ella Fitzgerald, and Sarah Vaughn. Produced by the famous impresario Norman Granz, who eventually settled in Geneva in 1959, the concerts were among the first high-profile performances in Switzerland to feature racially integrated bands. I spent much time with the Modern Jazz Quartet and became very friendly with some of its musicians, particularly Percy Heath, Milt Jackson, and Connie Kay. I would meet them at the plane and take them to restaurants, introduce them around, and translate for them.

Delphine gave birth to our daughter Annelle in January 1956, and we moved into a larger, two-bedroom apartment. Geneva was a wonderful place to have a baby. When my wife and Annelle came home from the hospital, our Swiss neighbors had prepared food for us. I'll never forget it. The university even forgave my tuition for a semester. But when Annelle came down with rheumatic fever in 1957, Delphine and I decided that she and the baby should go back to the States. Delphine returned with Annelle to Fayetteville and started teaching again.

During the next two and a half years, I split my time between my medical studies in Geneva and my home life in the United States. During part of one summer, I remained in Geneva to study after failing an exam in biochemistry. The professor had asked a simple question in French that I misunderstood. I repeated the course again six months later and passed, but studying in a foreign language introduced many such obstacles.

As part of our medical training, we were required to arrange three short externships to gain practical experience. The hospitals were generally happy for extra help that was unpaid, and they provided room and board. During spring break of 1956, I spent about a month at the old hospital in Grimsby, a fishing port on the northeast coast of England. There I worked in the internal medicine ward and the emergency room, frequently repairing wounds. Overall, it was an incredible experience. I was treated well and learned a lot. That summer, I was an extern at Montefiore Hospital in the Bronx. In the summer of 1957, at Morrisiana Hospital in the Bronx, I worked in the OB/GYN section. We delivered hundreds of babies at all times of the day and night, and I found it exciting. One diagnosis I made saved a woman's life. She had developed an ectopic pregnancy that was misdiagnosed by other physicians, who had sent her home. When she returned to the hospital, I diagnosed her correctly, whereupon she was rushed to the operating room and operated on successfully.

In Switzerland, medical students are granted a *Certificat de fin d'études médicales* upon completion of their studies and then must spend years in a hospital receiving further training. American students are required to earn an MD degree to practice in the States. After passing final exams, I had to write a thesis to earn the *Diplome de Docteur* in medicine. The head of the department would propose a project; the student would do the research; and finally, the head of the department would either approve or reject the work.

My thesis was *De L'influence de la morphine et de la chlorpromazine sur l'hyperthermie et l'hypothermie provoquees par des causes physiques chez le cobaye* (The Influence of Morphine and Chlorpromazine on Hyperthermia and Hypothermia Provoked by Physical Causes on Guinea Pigs). I concluded that both morphine (an analgesic and narcotic drug) and chlorpromazine (a synthetic drug used as a tranquilizer and sedative and to prevent vomiting) worsen the harmful effects on guinea pigs of exposure to heatstroke and frostbite.

In December 1959, after having been granted the *Certificat de fin d'etudes medicales*, I received my *Diplome de Docteur* in medicine and boarded a plane home, eager to see my wife and daughter in Fayetteville. Looking back, I'm overwhelmed by the kind of life we were able to live in Geneva. More importantly, I realized that the education I received there was better than any I might have received at most medical schools in America—in the rare event of admission as an African American. Just as an automobile accident had saved me from going to war in Korea, fate had again intervened. In being forced to go abroad, I gained excellent training and spent some of the happiest years of my life in Europe.

Conclusion

Fifteen years after returning to New York from Switzerland, I encountered one of the most difficult times in my life. On November 19, 1975, my wife, Annie Delphine Evans Primm, a warm, loving, intelligent woman, an extremely talented musician and teacher, died after a long and painful struggle with breast cancer. Few have had a larger funeral than Delphine's in New Rochelle. People streamed in, including Jerome Hornblass, the city official who had been our bitter enemy. He represented Mayor Beame.

Following a master's degree from the College of New Rochelle in music education for children with learning disabilities, Delphine had dedicated herself to this work. Somehow she found the time and energy to be a devoted mother, an elementary school teacher, a wife, and a choirmaster. I have never known anybody with a greater sense of responsibility of parenthood, and it wasn't until she became ill that I appreciated the extent of her devotion and accomplishments. At that point, I turned my attention to my three daughters who were at the time twelve, sixteen, and twenty years old. Jeanine was in middle school, Martine in high school, and Annelle in premed at Harvard. Their mother's death was shattering, and I was frequently away, leaving the girls in the care of housekeepers to manage as best we could. "Our whole world crumbled," recalled Martine. "When my mother was alive, our house was filled with music." I was left struggling to fill an unfillable gap in their lives and found wanting. Jeanine remembers that they "never left their rooms the first Christmas," and added that she felt the loss of parental love with her mother's death. She is convinced that I had been raised without much physical show of affection, leaving me unable to show love. Now, I had to learn. Over time, she believes, I've "grown softer, like a gentle giant."

The nature of my work in addiction treatment had troubled Delphine early on, and she opposed it. But as she saw my growing determination and commitment, she relented. It was what I wanted. On this subject, Martine believes that I have "an underdog syndrome," leading me to show affection more easily to people outside the family—addicts, for example.

But as she has watched me open up, she understands that I have loved my family deeply all along.

In the years following Delphine's death, Barbara Gibson, a clinical social worker who had come to ARTC in the early 1970s, became increasingly important in my life. Barbara and I first met at Interfaith Hospital where she was a part-time counselor while attending Queens College. She became my personal assistant at ARTC and eventually the second love of my life. Barbara was warm, beautiful, and outgoing, with a wry sense of humor, someone whom people gravitated toward. Barbara and I were suited to each other and enjoyed an excellent long-term relationship. One of the greatest mistakes in my life was not marrying her. She would have made a wonderful wife.

Barbara was a ready-to-lie-down-in-front-of-bulldozers revolutionary and had earlier joined me in occupying buildings. (Andrew Goodman, one of the young Civil Rights workers killed in 1964 in Mississippi, had been Barbara's classmate.) But what almost killed her was random gun violence. One hot summer evening in 1977, she left our headquarters in Brooklyn and drove to her apartment at Rochdale Village in Jamaica, Queens. As she was parking her Mustang, a guy stuck a gun through the open window and said, "Give me your pocketbook." As she threw the bag up at him, he fired his gun. The bullet left a tunnel wound through her liver and damaged her spleen and pancreas. The attack against Barbara brought to mind the famous case of Kitty Genovese, who had died in 1964 when no one in the surrounding buildings, having watched her brutal assault, came to her aid. Similarly, Barbara crawled out of her car and stumbled along the sidewalk looking for help. A man parking his car called to her, "Did your boyfriend do it?" and then walked away. People waiting at a bus stop ignored her. After half an hour, someone flagged down a security guard, and she was taken to Queens General Hospital. Dr. Harold Freeman, the director of the Department of Surgery at Harlem Hospital, and Dr. Herbert Cave, my mentor and chief of anesthesiology at Harlem Hospital, rushed to Queens General at my request, where they had no affiliation, to perform the eight-hour surgery that saved her life. Barbara was in the hospital for a month. Had she not been a robust woman, she surely would have died. Tragically, it was a freak and careless car accident twenty-two years later that took Barbara's life.

"I remember my father at Barbara's funeral," recalls my daughter Martine, "throwing the last flower into her grave."

Today, I am fortunate to have four wonderful daughters, three from my marriage to Delphine and one, Eraka, from a relationship with physician colleague and ophthalmologist Dr. Patricia Bath. I have two granddaughters, India and Noa. My daughters are all accomplished, professional women. Annelle B. Primm, who was born in Geneva, is deputy medical director of the American Psychiatric Association and in charge of minority mental health programs for the organization. Martine was a member of the American Stock Exchange and is currently a flight attendant. Jeanine Primm Jones is a counselor and artist. Eraka Bath Fortuit is a psychiatrist.

A family friendship that began almost fifty years ago evolved into a love for my fiancée, Ellena Stone Huckaby Through good times and through times of family tragedy, our relationship has deepened and filled a void in our lives. I came to love Ellena for her inner and outer beauty, her intellect, her compassion for others, and for her spirit and courage.

Entering Fisk University at the age of fourteen on a Ford Foundation scholarship, Ellena studied under Harlem Renaissance icons Aaron Douglas, Arna Bontemps, and Langston Hughes. A native of Houston, Texas, she was a governor's appointee to the Texas Committee for the Humanities, a founding member of the Houston Museum of African American Culture, and a city commissioner for the arts. She currently serves as a curator of several collections and maintains a consulting firm in art and interior design in New York.

My interest in art has been complemented by her passion and knowledge of African American arts and culture. Her involvement in my work, particularly in efforts combating HIV/AIDS, led to an unusual marrying of the arts with health-related projects and philanthropic activities. In addition, we share a global perspective on other issues, including a push worldwide for the education of girls and for social justice.

Lookingback, I have been blessed during the last fifteen years to have Ellena as my loving companion. And now we share a lifetime of stories to pass on to my two and Ellena's six grandchildren.

Epilogue

*We should go forward, groping our way through the
darkness, stumbling perhaps at times, and try to do what good
lay in our power.*

Albert Camus, *The Plague*

I was drawn to drug abuse treatment fifty years ago as a young doctor witnessing black men in Harlem Hospital destroying their lives through drug abuse. I and my colleagues in the field have traveled a long distance from the major discoveries of the 1960s by Vincent Dole and Marie Nyswander at the Rockefeller Institute, who proved that addiction was indeed a disease. Soon after, we entered a period of fear and condemnation of addicts, epitomized by Governor Rockefeller's law and order approach of lock 'em up and throw away the key. Today, we have at long last seen the dawn of enlightened attitudes toward addicted individuals as well as toward the increasingly discredited war on drugs. In 2011, The Global Commission on Drug Policy released a report concluding that the "global war on drugs has failed, with devastating consequences for individuals and societies around the world." The commission, which included such heavy hitters as former UN Secretary-General Kofi Annan, former US Secretary of State George P. Schultz, and former US Federal Reserve chairman Paul Volcker, stated that the United States must change its antidrug policies from an anticrime approach to a focus on healthcare and human rights. An article on the *Forbes* website in the spring of 2012 was more direct: "The drug war is insane. We are no safer, and we are certainly less free because of concerted efforts to wage war on drugs. It's time to stop the insanity."

I have long believed that we should devote our resources to the treatment of mental illness and the other health problems that are both the cause and effect of drug addiction. In addition, the social stigma and racial discrimination intertwined with addiction are social ills that cry out for an aggressive and sustained response.

In fewer than thirty years, the prison population in the United States has exploded from about 300 thousand to more than two million. Drug convictions account for the majority of the increase. "In major cities wracked by the drug war, as many as 80 percent of young African American men now have criminal records and are thus subject to legalized discrimination for the rest of their lives," Michelle Alexander writes in her powerful book *The New Jim Crow*. "Today, the War on Drugs has given birth to a system of mass incarceration that governs not just a small fraction of a racial or ethnic minority but entire communities of color."

In the case of marijuana, we see some change. Beyond the few states that have legalized marijuana for medical purposes, referendums in Washington and Colorado in the fall of 2012 made marijuana legal for purely recreational use. My position on this drug is yes to availability for medical purposes with careful prior evaluation, no to an open, indiscriminate availability. Marijuana is extremely addictive, and its abuse leads to serious motivational problems causing students to fail and employees to lose their jobs.

While it remains illegal, I still believe that someone who sells marijuana should face criminal penalties, but I am not in favor of criminal penalties for possession. Decriminalization would end the police practice of frisking and arresting people for carrying small amounts of the drug, a policy that affects blacks and Latinos disproportionately.

Saddling kids, from high school dropouts to college graduates, with criminal records that keep them from getting jobs, credit cards, and rental apartments would also stop with decriminalization. An acquaintance was recently arrested after police found a small amount of marijuana in her car. Now, even with a master's degree, she can't find a job.

I strongly oppose dispensaries, of which a growing number have appeared, that make such analgesics as oxycontin and methadone easily available. It is one thing to seek the relief of pain and another to seek euphoria, an addictive feeling leading to drug addiction. I'm hopeful that the new healthcare law will put an end to these pill mills and the easy availability of methadone, now the cheapest painkiller available.

In 2012, the Centers for Disease Control and Prevention reported that methadone contributed to more than 30 percent of deaths from an overdose of prescription painkillers, although the drug accounted for only 2 percent of the country's pain prescriptions. As CDC Director Dr. Thomas Frieden explained, "Methadone used for heroin substitution treatment does not appear to be a major part of this problem. However, the amount of methadone prescribed to people in pain has increased dramatically." Doctors prescribe methadone because it costs a couple of dollars less per tablet than other painkillers such as Vicodin and Oxycontin.

In the future, I believe, less addictive options such as buprenorphine and suboxone will become more widely available. Suboxone can be implanted subcutaneously to block the euphoric effects of heroin and is more easily controlled than methadone. These options represent promising avenues for future treatment and will bring about a decrease in the prison population as addicts receive treatment instead of jail time. Overall, a new mindset is gradually taking hold as the laws governing substance abuse become less draconian and as we see strides in the rehabilitation of the addicted. It is a change in attitude that was unimaginable fifty years ago.

For the first time in our history, the number of patients at our clinics recently has dropped considerably. Since 2009 when we served over two thousand people, we have seen a decrease of 10 percent. This decrease can be explained by the easy availability of methadone and other substances that can now be obtained legally—though often through providers who lack training in pain management. In addition, it appears that fewer people are abusing than before because drug prices on the street have risen and now consume a greater proportion of a shrinking budget for food and shelter. Also, the stop and frisk policy has made people more wary of the criminal justice system.

ARTC and other treatment centers are at a disadvantage in the area of grants and federal funds, which, when given to universities, usually include an overhead or cost rate that can be as much as 50 percent. Funders, however, are often reluctant to pay our overhead rates, and so our costs must be deducted from funds that should support services. Finally, the downturn in the economy has led to decreased federal grants to providers such as ARTC, and New York State has changed its reimbursement policy to providers as well.

* * *

On May 1, 2012, I reluctantly retired after forty-three years as executive director of ARTC, now known as START treatment and recovery centers, remaining as a special advisor to the CEO. At the age of eighty-four, with my health deteriorating, I decided it was time to hand my responsibilities on to a younger leader, Dr. Lawrence Brown, who was a senior executive vice president. He became the permanent executive director of ARTC, while the Urban Resource Institute board selected Nathaniel Fields, a senior vice president of domestic violence programs for Safe Horizon, an organization that aids victims of domestic abuse. URI officially separated from ARTC on July 1, 2012. As a result, more than sixty people retired or lost their jobs. They include senior vice president Deborah Wright, who arranged the conversion and restoration of the buildings that today form the basis of the organization's endowment; Vice President Robert Sage, director of human services; Vice President Eddie Lightsey, director of the finance division; Vice President Angela Grant, director of HIV prevention and intervention services; and my longtime and devoted assistant Maxine Dotson.

A grandson of a slave, I have been privileged during the course of my life to work with our nation's presidents, to advise foreign governments, and to serve as a healer those with broken lives. Gerald Warfield, for instance, now retired from ARTC, came to us for treatment in 1984 after over fifteen years of heroin, cocaine, and alcohol abuse as well as of "reds"—methamphetamine, tuinals, and Quaaludes. Gerald had finally turned to crime—armed robbery, breaking and entering—to support a habit that was costing him nearly $300 a day. Soon after his start in counseling in Narcotics Anonymous at our Fort Greene clinic, he began methadone treatment and stopped using heroin. Within about a year, Gerald ended methadone treatment, remained drug free, and joined us as a security guard. Ultimately, he was promoted to group specialist and counselor to run a Narcotics Anonymous Group at our clinics.

"Going to ARTC was the best thing that ever happened to me," he recounted. "Methadone allowed me to be stable and to spring into a drug-free lifestyle. Being an addict was the worst job I ever had. And I didn't have the resources to quit by myself." In many of our clinic rooms where Gerald meets his groups, the twelve steps of Narcotics Anonymous are posted. On the wall of one group room is Reinhold Niebuhr's Serenity Prayer: "God grant me the serenity to accept the things I cannot change, the courage to change the things I can, and the wisdom to know the difference."

My own belief in God goes hand in hand with my acceptance of an obligation to live a righteous life. I have fought two plagues afflicting the United States at the end of the twentieth century and into the twenty-first: drug abuse and HIV/AIDS. From the first days of ARTC, a framed poster of Dr. Martin Luther King Jr. shaking hands with Malcolm X has hung prominently at our headquarters. These two men represent the divergent ways in which I have worked to serve black Americans. After fifty years in the trenches, I have quit the field of battle, but I have not given up the fight. I will continue to work against injustice and the neglect of the least of us.

From the day my mother packed me into her Chevrolet to drive from Williamson to New York, fate and force of will have guided me toward my true north, fulfilling the dreams of a small boy playing doctor in his father's funeral home.

Notes and Sources

Chapter One

the hospital was lily-white: Telephone interview with John Anderson, August 9, 2011.

all out war on drugs and addiction: Edward Jay Epstein, *Agency of Fear* (G. P. Putnam's Sons, New York, 1977), pp. 38-39.

half the crime in New York City: Ibid., pp. 39-40.

he didn't want to use drugs anymore: Telephone interview with Danny Cook, May 11, 2011.

There is only one rehabilitation center in Harlem: Sidney Zion, "Narcotics Aides Scored in Harlem,"New York Times, July 25, 1968.

the zeal of a country preacher: George Vecsey, "Thomas Matthew: A Man Under Fire,"New York Times, April 24, 1973.

given a neurosurgeon's ratings: Ibid.

with initial funding from churches: Telephone interview with Carol and Laura Matthew, March 16, 2012.

drug capital of America: "Harlem History 1658 to the Present," *Harlem World Magazine,* http://harlemworldmag.com/2011/07/02/harlem-history-1658-to-present/

who himself had received treatment: Telephone interview with Reverend James Allen, April 16, 2012

Mayor John Lindsay found himself caught: Thomas A. Johnson, "12 are Arrested Here: Sporadic Violence Erupts in Harlem,"New York Times, April 5, 1968.

at four o'clock: Martin Gansberg, "12 Sit in At Governor's Office to Protest Hospital Aid Cut,"New York Times, April 8, 1968.

introduced them when Nixon was practicing law: George Vecsey, "Thomas Matthew:
A Man Under Fire,"New York Times, April 24, 1973.

Tom was able to obtain: Ibid.

"from somebody in the White House": Ibid.

"all assistance possible": Paul Delaney, " 'All Assistance Possible' to Matthew Reported Ordered Personally by Nixon,"New York Times, December 11, 1973.

Alton Marshall: Ralph Blumenthal, "Rockefeller Aide Helped Hospital,"New York Times, December 5, 1974.

"leaned over backwards": Ibid.

pardoned by Nixon: Robert Semple Jr., "Nixon Frees Leader of Negro Self-Help Unit,"New York Times, January 6, 1970.

was sentenced to three years: Will Lissner, "Dr. Matthew Given a 3-Year Sentence,"New York Times, December 27, 1973.

not one fragment: Robert D. McFadden, "Court Reverses Matthew Verdict,"New York Times, March 4, 1975.

Chapter Two

badly troubled, with self-destructive drives: Laurie Johnston, "Heroin-Maintenance Proponent,"New York Times, May 11, 1972.

Drugs and crime were exploding: Interview with Jay Kriegel, September 5, 2011.

"good government" individuals: Robert G. Newman, asterisk note, *Methadone Treatment in Narcotic Addiction* (Academic Press, New York, 1977), p. 6.

the federal government first became involved: Nancy D. Campbell, JP Olsen, Luke Walden, *The Narcotic Farm: The Rise and Fall of America's First Prison for Drug Addicts* (Abrams, New York, n.d.), p. 15.

the term addict was defined: The National Alliance of Advocates for Buprenorphine Treatment, http://www.naabt.org/glossary.cfm.

on the one hand: Nancy D. Campbell, JP Olsen, Luke Walden, *The Narcotic Farm* (Abrams, New York, n.d.), p. 12.

art, music therapy: Jana Burson, Janaburson's blog,

William S. Burroughs: Charles Q. Choi, "Reaping a Sad Harvest: A Narcotic Farm that Tried to Grow Recovery," *Scientific American* http://www.scientificamerican.com/article.cfm?id=narcotics-recovery-farm.

the best jazz band in the world: "America's First Drug-Treatment Prison Revisited," NPR, November 1, 2008.

first synthesized in 1937: Ralf Gerlach, "The History of Methadone," http://www.indro-online.de/historymethadone.htm.

"We had no beginning template": William L. White, "Edward C. Senay, M.D.: Lessons From Four Decades of Clinical Practice," *Counselor*, February 2011, http://www.williamwhitepapers.com/pr/2011%20Dr.%20Edward%20Senay.pdf.

"the group of people who were then young": Telephone interview with Dr. Robert Dupont, December 12, 2011.

Vincent Paul Dole Jr.: "Vincent P. Dole," The Rockefeller University, http://www.rockefeller.edu/about/awards/lasker/vdole.

Marie Nyswander: "Marie Nyswander," Wikipedia, http://en.wikipedia. org/wiki/Marie_Nyswander.

Journal of the American Medical Association: Vincent P. Dole and Marie Nyswander, "A Medical Treatment for Diacetylmorphine (Heroin) Addiction: A Clinical Trial With Methadone Hydrochloride," *JAMA*, 193 (8), 1965, pp. 646-650.

In a related article: Vincent P. Dole, Marie Nyswander and Mary Jeanne Kreek, "Narcotic Blockade: A Medical Technique for Stopping Heroin Use by Addicts," *Transactions of the Association of American Physicians*, 79, 1966, pp. 122-136.

Dole wrote a letter: Vincent P. Dole, letter to Herbert Sturz, May 1969.

"These schmucks had the chutzpah": Interview with Herman Joseph, May 22, 2012.

Real expansion: Kriegel.

I told the Doles: Interview with Herbert Sturz, August 23, 2011.

wrote a memo in March 1969: Mitchell Ginsberg and Bernard Bucove, "Methadone Proposal Memo to John Lindsay," The City of New York Human Resources Administration, March 28, 1969.

home in Riverdale: Interview with Nicholas deB. Katzenbach, August 24, 2011.

Chapter Three

largest methadone program: Charlayne Hunter, "New Brooklyn Addicts Center Relies on Methadone and Advice,"New York Times, *October 12, 1969.*

In the beginning, Brooklyn was rough: Interviews with Tom Rafalsky, September 28, 2011, October 12, 2011, and January 18, 2012.

giving too much drugs: Richard Severo, "Rumor, Intrigue and Criticism Beset City's Brooklyn Methadone Center; Methadone Clinic is Under Attack,"New York Times, June 11, 1970.

plague of narcotics: "Lindsay Inaugurates a Methadone Center,"New York Times, December 1, 1970.

the methadone capital of the world: New York Daily News, March 12, 1973.

people would simply get medicated: Interview with Robert Sage, May 11, 2011.

Modest Help for a Few: Irving P. Lukoff and James Vorenberg, "Methadone Maintenance—Modest Help for a Few," Center for Socio-Cultural Studies on Drug Use, Columbia University School of Social Work, December 1975, p. 23.

seminal study: John C. Ball and Alan Ross, *The Effectiveness of Methadone Maintenance Treatment* (Springer-Verlag, New York, 1991).

Chapter Four

his entire generation: Michael Massing, *The Fix* (University of California Press, Berkeley, California, 2000), p. 97.

as motorists have to gasoline: Edward Jay Epstein, *Agency of Fear* (G. P. Putnam's Sons, New York, 1977) p. 126.

disturbing news: Massing, p. 107.

piss in a bottle: Massing, p. 110.

public enemy: Richard Nixon, "Remarks About an Intensified Program for Drug Abuse Prevention and Control," The American Presidency Project, June 17, 1971, http://www.presidency.ucsb.edu/ws/?pid=3047.

the President called me into his cabinet room: Telephone interview with Dr. Jerome Jaffe, May 13, 2011.

250,000 to 600,000: Massing, p. 113.

kick some tail: Drug Wars," Produced by Brooke Runnette and Martin Smith, PBS, *Frontline*, first aired, October 9, 2000.

Code of Military Justice: Ibid., p. 114.

behind black colleges: Epstein, p. 154.

two firms that had expressed interest: Ibid., p. 155.

Who could have predicted": John W. Finney, "Study Finds Few Veterans Are Addicted to Drugs,"New York Times, April 24, 1973.

"half the men addicted in Vietnam": Lee N. Robins, "Vietnam Veterans Rapid Recover From Heroin Addiction: A Fluke or Normal Expectation?" *Addiction* (88) 1993, p. 1046.

Chapter Five

"constant harassment": David C. Berliner, "Park Slope Protesting Number of Drug Centers," New York Times, October 7, 1973.

if the community is unstable: Ibid.

Dr. Primm has done a fine job: Ibid.

very valuable: Ibid.

I discussed the transition: New York Amsterdam News, August 18, 1973.

lacked the kind of programmatic: Telephone interview with Jerome Hornblass, June 6, 2012.

it was a nightmare: Interview with Mitchell Rosenthal, February 1, 2012.

"misuse of large sums of money": Edward Hudson, "Group Asks a City Drug Aide to Resign," New York Times, August 9, 1974.

not to be evidence of fraud: Ibid.

deficiencies and questionable practices: Edith Evans Asbury, "Brooklyn Group
Urges Inquiry at Methadone Center," New York Times, November 7, 1974.

defending us: Ibid.

we worked for five days: Interview with Maxine Dotson, November 30, 2011.

Chapter Six

you must be crazy: Interview with Loraine Madry, December 20, 2011.

$500,000 over the years: Telephone interview with Carmen Smith, August 23, 2013.

They told me what to do: Interview with "Rosa," November 30, 2011.

exclusive hard-to-crack social groups: Lawrence Otis Graham, *Our Kind of People: Inside America's Black Upper Class* (Harper Perennial, New York, 2000), p. 15.

"an integral part of life and culture": Robert Hayden, *African Americans on Martha's Vineyard* (Select Publications, Boston, Mass., 2005), p. xiii.

On the Vineyard people often nod or wave to me when I driveby in my vintage car, a replica of a 1931 Ford Phaeton Abercrombie Runabout. It's a red convertible with white sidewalls. I've had it for forty years.

Chapter Seven

the most important spokesman: Telephone interview with Peter Bourne, March 19, 2012.

Len Bias: Rick Weinberg," Len Bias Dies of Cocaine Overdose," ESPN. com,,http://sports.espn.go.com/espn/espn25/story?page=moments/34.

given a blank check: Interview with Lisa Tatum Scheckel Levy, July 18, 2011.

"created a framework": Interview with Sue Becker, July 18, 2011.

Chapter Eight

Haitians: http://pathmicro.med.sc.edu/spanish-virology/4hclub.htm.

One theory: Roger Highfield, "AIDS study showed that it arrived in US in 1960's," *The Telegraph,* London, October 29, 2007.

people were dying within six months: Telephone interview with Elaine Greeley, July 10, 2012.

I will be heard: "Timeline: Thirty Years of AIDS in Black America," Frontline, PBS, July 10, 2012, http://www.pbs.org/wgbh/pages/frontline/social-issues/endgame-aids-in-black-america/timeline-30-years-of-aids-in-black-america/.

fifteen minutes but Koop: p. 214-215.
Ibid.

treatment on demand: Report of the Presidential Commission on the Human Immunodeficiency Virus Epidemic, June 24, 1988, p. 95.

men who engaged: Samuel R. Friedman, Don des Jarlais, Jo L. Sotheran, and Rand Stoneburner, "The Sharing of Drug Injection Equipment and the AIDS Epidemic in New York City: The First Decade," NIDA Research Monograph 1988 (80), pp. 160-175. Reprinted on Believer's Web, http://www.believersweb.org/view.cfm?ID=520.

Do I wish I could have done more?: Lawrence K. Altman, "Clinton Urges Global Planning to Halt H.I.V.," New York Times, July 12, 2002.
It took so long: Telephone interview with Paul Kawata, January 10, 2012.

As the CDC meeting began on March 8: For many of the following details of this meeting and of my subsequent activities in Washington regarding AIDS, I have refreshed my memory by relying on Jacob Levenson's superb account in his *The Secret Epidemic: The Story of AIDS in Black America* (Anchor, New York, 2005).

racist agenda: Ibid., p. 224.

sense of urgency: Ibid., p. 224.

but they account for about fifty-seven percent: Sheryl Gay Stolberg, "Epidemic of Silence: A Special Report.; Eyes Shut, Black America Is Being Ravaged by AIDS,"New York Times, June 29, 1998.

who had known me: Levenson, p. 225.

subsidized addiction and death: Ibid., p. 214.

held a meeting: Other members of the Congressional Black Caucus in attendance included Donna Christian-Christensen, Barbara Lee, Sheila Jackson Lee, and Eleanor Holmes Norton.

a state of emergency: Letter from Maxine waters, chair of the Congressional Black Caucus to Donna Shalala, Secretary of Health and Human Services, May 13, 1998.

had to be understood more broadly: Levenson, p. 232.

epidemic of silence: Stolberg, Ibid.

outside our traditional purview: Levenson, p. 233.

Julian Bond: Ibid., p. 233.

Helen Gayle called: Ibid., p. 234.

Don't you dare: Ibid., p. 234.

or perhaps even racist: Ibid., p. 236.

"like other epidemics before it,*"* Ibid., p. 237.

biting his lip: Ibid.

this milestone today: Donna Shalala, "Responding to the Crisis," HHS. Government Archive, October 28, 1998.

approximately $367 million: Aids funding, blog.AIDS.gov., http://blog. aids.gov/2011/05/evolutions-in-the-minority-aids-initiative-secretary's-fund.html.

traditionally black churches: Jennifer Steinhauer, "Shift in Money and Message As Minorities Take On AIDS," New York Times, December 17, 1999.

represented a community: Interview with Dr. Mary Jeanne Kreek, October 3, 2012.

came to realize the humanity: Interview with Jeanine Primm, July 13, 2011.

named Mike Sisco: The Oprah Winfrey Show AIDS in Williamson, West Virginia, November 16, 1987, http://www.oprah.com/oprahshow/ AIDS-Comes-to-a-Small-Town#ixzz2gKgVbGQz.

later in 2010: The Oprah Winfrey Show 23 Years Later: Oprah Returns to Williamson, West Virginia, September 15, 2010, http:// www.oprah.com/oprahshow/Oprah-Returns-to-Williamson-West-Virginia/3#ixzz2gKcBW76h.

Chapter Nine

Matewan massacre: Rebecca J. Bailey, *Matewan Before the Massacre: Politics, Coal, and the Roots of Conflict in a West Virginia Mining*

Community (West Virginia University Press, Morgantown, West Virginia, 2008), pp. 5-7.

Cinderella movie theater: Telephone interviews with C. Travis Fulghan, July 22, 2011 and August 8, 2011.

blacks in the Mountain State: "Race, Class and Industrial Change: Black Migration to Southern West Virginia, 1915-1932," *The Great Migration in Historical Perspective: New Dimensions of Race, Class & Gender*, ed. by Joe William Trotter, Jr., (Indiana University Press, Bloomington and Indianapolis, 1991), p. 62.

He didn't take nothin': Telephone interview with Alvin Leonard, July 20, 2011.

Williamson's population: City of Williamson, http://www.williamsonwest-virginia.us/Personal%20Web%20Page.htm#_Biographical_Information, and US Census Bureau, Google.com/Public Data, http://www.google.com/publicdata/explore?ds=kf7tgg1uo9ude_&met_y=population&idim=place:5487508&dl=en&hl=en&q=population%20of%20williamson,%20west%20virginia.

over the course of six decades: Isabel Wilkerson, *The Warmth of Other Suns: The Epic Story of America's Great Migration* (Random House, New York, 2010), p. 9.

Their migration was a response: Ibid., pp. 14-15.

a parent or grandparent: Ibid., p. 10.

Chapter Ten

brimming with great energy: "Harlem in the 1940's," PBS, http://www.pbs.org/hollywoodpresents/theoldsettler/about/about_harlem.html

called the Black Eagle: Betty Kaplan Gubert, Miriam Sawyer, and Caroline M. Fannin, *Distinguished African Americans in Aviation and Space Science* (Greenwood, no city listed, 2001) p. 185.

hip-hop was born in the West Bronx: David Gonzalez, "Will Gentrification Spoil the Birthplace of Hip-Hop?" New York Times, May 21, 2007.

our own little Bethlehem: Jennifer 8 Lee, "An Effort to Honor the Birthplace of Hip-Hop," New York Times, July 23, 2007.

She ran everything: Telephone interview with Gloria Primm Brown, March 5, 2012.

largest high school in the world: Gerard J. Pelisson and James A. Garvey III, *The Castle on the Parkway: The Story of New York City's Dewitt Clinton High School and its Extraordinary Influence on American Life* (The Hutch Press Scarsdale, N.Y., 2009), p. 68.

restricted blacks: Brian McKinney, "The Fight for Integration of Restaurants," Don's Maryland History, http://donsmarylandhistory.wikispaces.com/Restaurants+and+Integration+by+BM.

Bickford's, Ibid.

their father was a Baptist minister: John William Tuohy and Ed Becker, "The Legend of Tommy Roe," Americanmafia.com http://www.americanmafia.com/Feature_Articles_53.html

my nickname is listed as shorty: 1944 Yearbook Dewitt Clinton High School (Bronx, N. Y.) p. 59.
Rev. John Miller Dickey: "Lincoln University," BlackPast.org, http://www.blackpast.org/?q=aah/lincoln-university-1854.

This was the first institution: "About Lincoln," Lincoln University of the Commonwealth of Pennsylvania, http://www.lincoln.edu/about.html.

Notable alumni: "Lincoln University Pennsylvania," NNDB, Tracking the Entire World, http://www.nndb.com/edu/535/000102229/.

George Washington, http://en.wikipedia.org/wiki/West_Virginia_State_Universty
segregated public schools, Ibid

it belonged to a family named Cabbel: "West Virginia State," http://en.wikipedia.org/wiki/West_Virginia_State_University.

black colleges and universities: Kenneth E. Redd, "Historically Black Colleges and Universities: Making a Comeback," http://www.jessicapettitt.com/images/Merisotis.pdf.

Chapter Eleven

Truman's order: Harry S. Truman Library and Museum, Executive Order No. 9981, http://www.trumanlibrary.org/9981.htm.

Kenneth Clairborne Royall, "Origins of Executive Order 9981," Helium, http://www.helium.com/items/2085766-what-were-the-origins-of-executive-order-9981.

the prop blast is an airborne tradition: "Basic Airborne Course," The 506 Airborne Infantry Regiment Association, http://www.506infantry.org/hisabn/his2ndbnabnmemo03.html.

Triple Nickels, "Smokejumpers," Stormbringer,http://seanlinnane.blogspot.com/2012/01/smokejumpers.html

the Market House: Fred Whitted, *Fayetteville North Carolina* (Arcadia, Charleston, South Carolina, 2000), p. 11.

Chapter Twelve

Howard University was named after its founder: A Short History," Howard University College of Medicine, http://medicine.howard.edu/about/history/.

only other black medical school: George A. Johnston, Jr., "The Flexner Report and Black Medical Schools," *Journal of the National Medical Association*, vol. 76, no. 3, 1984, p. 223.

renamed the Meharry: Meharry Medical College, Wikipedia,http://en.wikipedia.org/wiki/Meharry_Medical_Collegep.

there was a quota: Rudolph Cumberbatch, *Failure Masquerading as Success* (AuthorHouse, Bloomington, Indiana, 2008) p. 88.

James McCune Smith: Thomas M. Morgan, "The Education and Medical Practice of Dr. James McCune Smith (1813-1865), First Black American to Hold Medical Degree," *Journal of the National Medical Association*, vol. 95, no. 7, July 2003, pp. 603-608.

Germany's oldest university: Euroscholars, http://www.euroscholars.eu/universities/ruprechtkarls.htm Heidelberg University.

forced sterilizations: "History of the University of Heidelberg," *Wikipedia*, http://en.wikipedia.org/wiki/History_of_the_University_of_Heidelberg,

The American model of race: Hanna Schissler, ed., *The Miracle Years: A Cultural History of West Germany, 1949-1968* (Princeton University Press, Princeton, New Jersey, 2001) p. 151.

At home in Alabama: Ibid, p. 153.

Granz, who eventually settled in Geneva in 1959: "Norman Granz," *Wikipedia*, http://en.wikipedia.org/wiki/Norman_Granz.

Conclusion

our whole world crumbled: Telephone interview with Martine Primm, November 23, 2011.

softer, like a gentle giant: Interview with Jeanine Primm, July 13, 2011.

Epilogue

the global war on drug has failed: War on Drugs: Report of the Global Commission on Drug Policy (Open Society Foundation, n.c., June 2011), p. 2.

the drug war is insane: Art Carden, "Let's Be Blunt: It's Time to End the Drug War," *Forbes*, April 19, 2012, http://www.forbes.com/sites/artcarden/2012/04/19/lets-be-blunt-its-time-to-end-the-drug-war/

has exploded from about 300,000 to more than two million: Michelle Alexander, *The New Jim Crow: Mass Incarceration in the Age of Colorblindness* (The New Press, New York, 2010), p. 6.

Methadone contributed to more: Press release, Centers for Disease Control and Prevention, July 3, 2012.http://www.cdc.gov/media/releases/2012/p0703_methadone.html.

being an addict was the worst job I ever had: Interview with Gerald Warfield, September 12, 2012.

Index

24518989R00116

Made in the USA
Middletown, DE
27 September 2015